PRODUCTION AND OPERATIONS MANAGEMENT

(First Edition)

Author

Asst. Prof. Ushma Vala

Head of the Department at Swami Sahajanand School of Management – Gujarat Technological University

(PhD*, CWM, MBA)

TABLE OF CONTENTS

Introduction, Nature, Scope and transformation Process of POM

BRIDGE (INTRODUCTION OF POM)

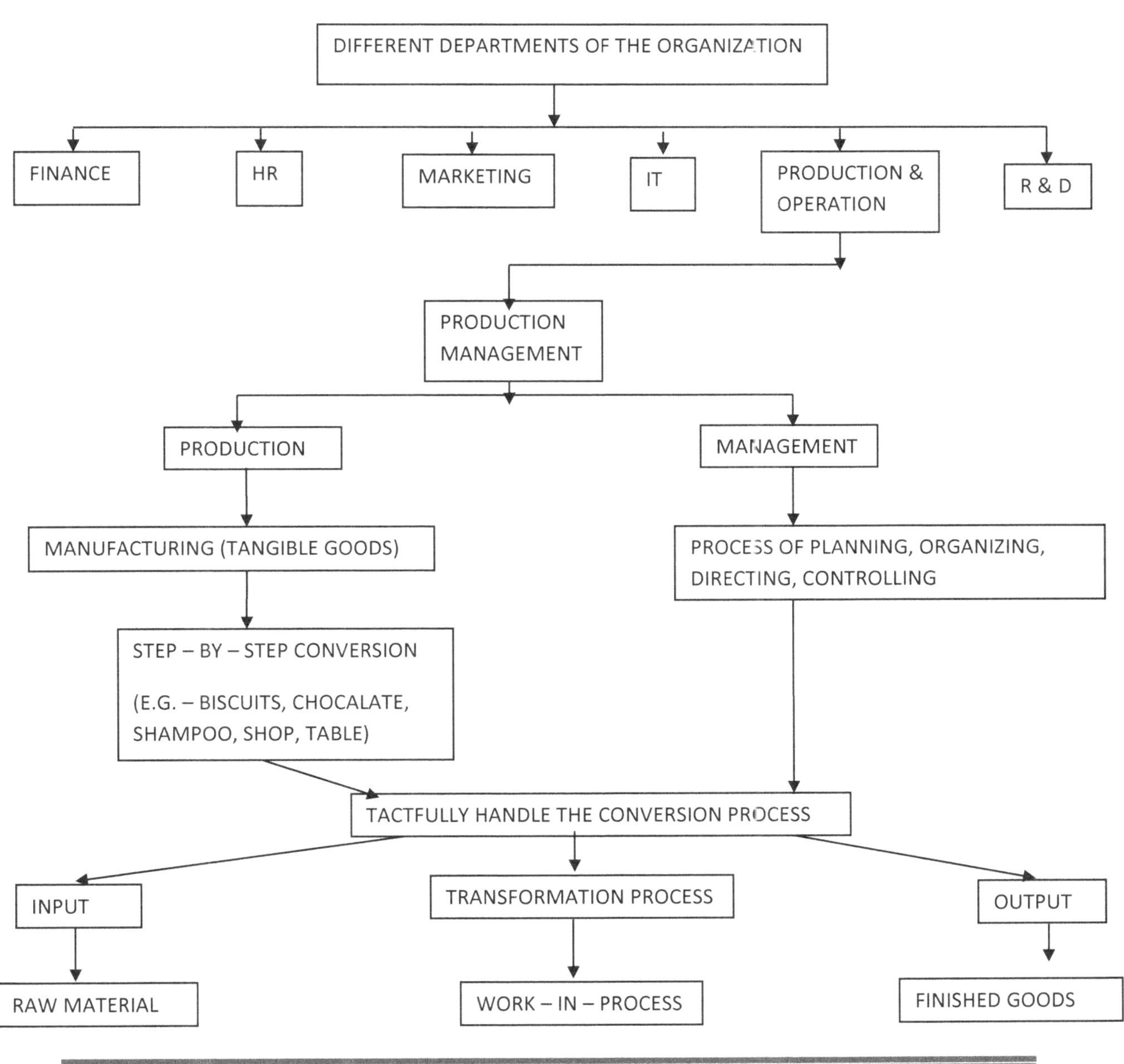

BRIDGE (WHY PRODUCTION MANAGEMENT)

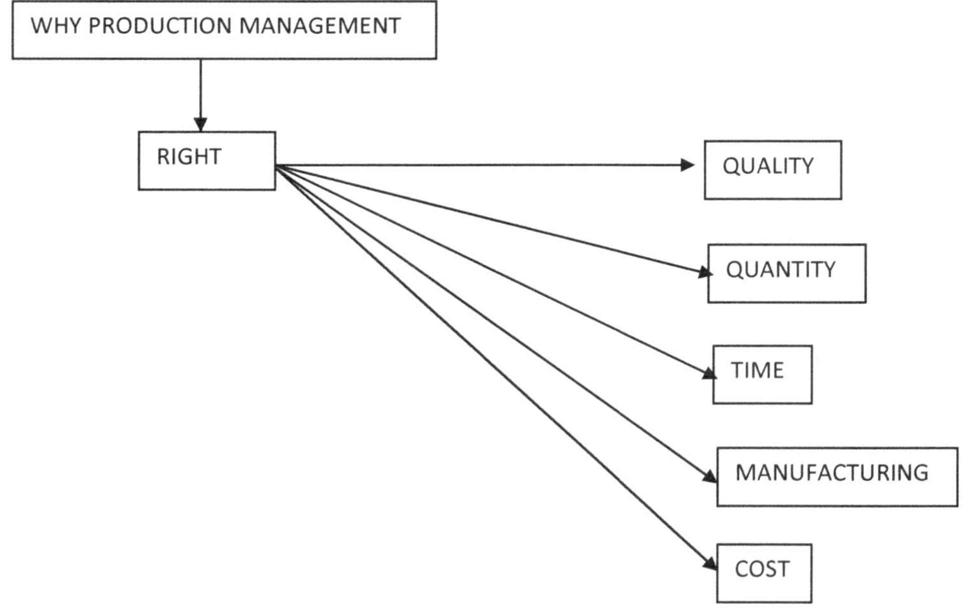

BRIDGE (OPERATION MANAGEMENT)

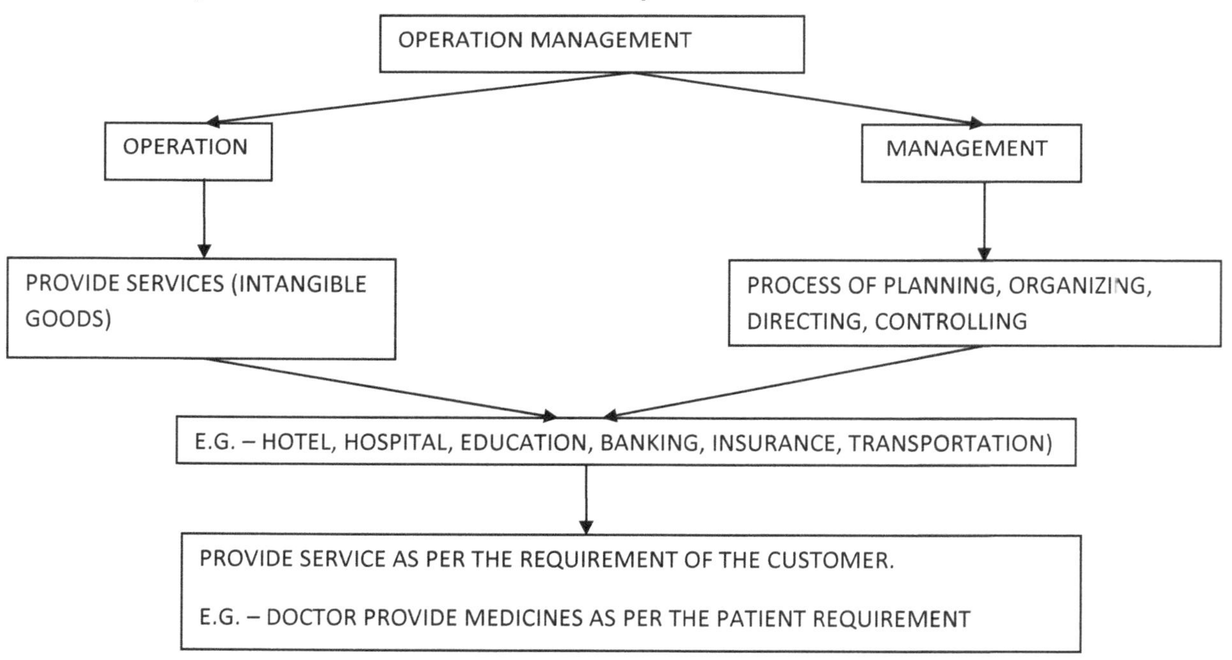

BRIDGE (SCOPE OF POM)

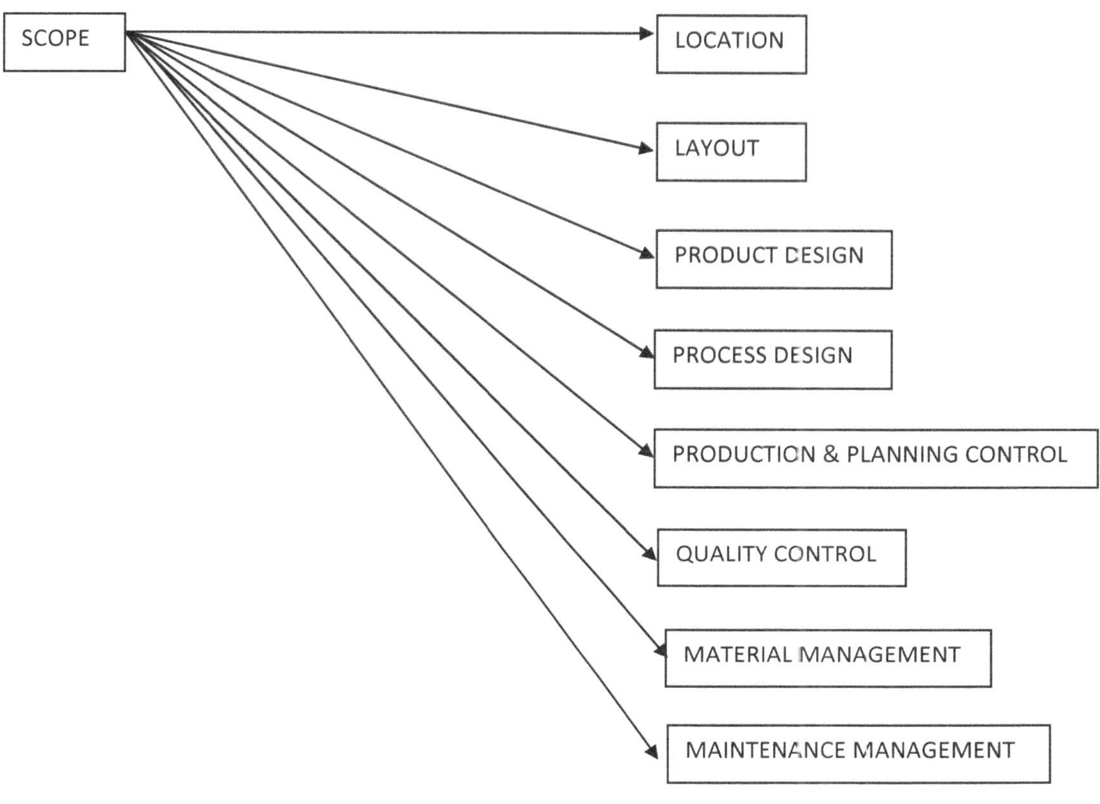

BRIDGE (BENEFITS DERIVED FROM EFFICIENT PRODUCTION MANAGEMENT)

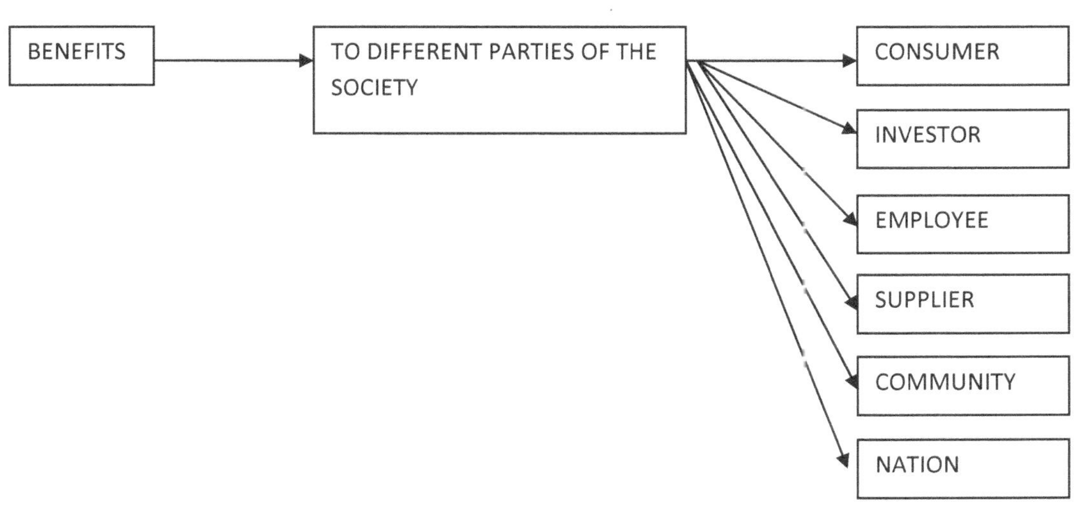

CONCEPT OF PRODUCTION

- Production function is that part of an organization, which is concerned with the **transformation** of a range of **inputs into the required outputs** (products) having the requisite quality level.

- Production is defined as *"the **step-by-step conversion** of one form of material into another form through chemical or mechanical process to create or enhance the utility of the product to the user."*

- Thus production is a value addition process.

- At each stage of processing, there will be value addition.

- Edwood Buffa defines production as *'a process by which goods and services are created'*.

- **Some examples of production are**: manufacturing custom-made products like, boilers with a specific capacity, constructing flats, some structural fabrication works for selected customers, etc., and manufacturing standardized products like, car, bus, motor cycle, radio, television, etc.

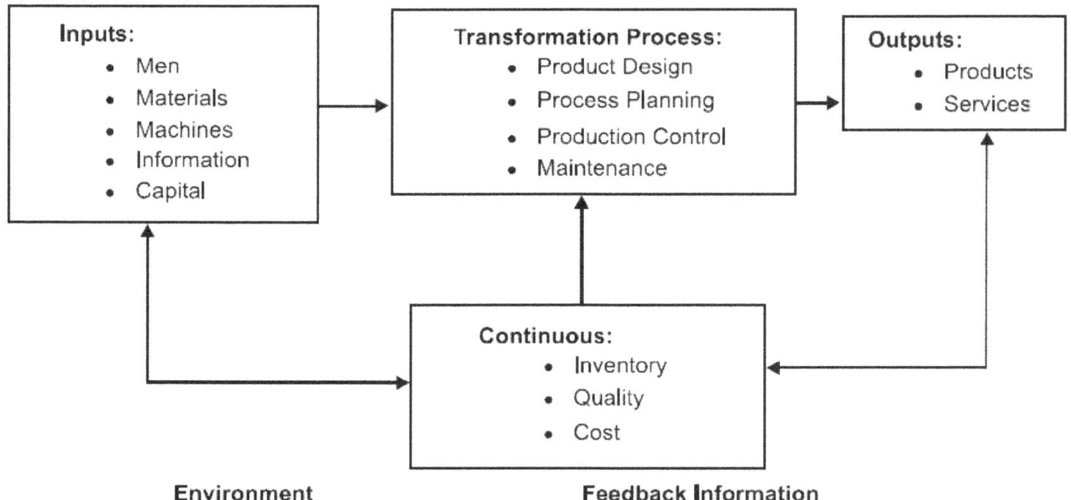

Fig. 1.1 *Schematic production system*

PRODUCTION MANAGEMENT

- Production management is a **process of planning, organizing, directing and controlling** the activities of the production function.

- It combines and transforms various resources used in the production subsystem of the organization into value added product in a controlled manner as per the policies of the organization.

- *E.S. Buffa* defines production management as, **"Production management** *deals with decision making related to production processes so that the resulting goods or services are produced according to specifications, in the amount and by the schedule demanded and out of minimum cost."*

Objectives of Production Management

The objective of the production management is 'to produce goods services of right quality and quantity at the right time and right manufacturing cost'.

1. RIGHT QUALITY

- The quality of product is established based upon the customers needs.

- The right quality is not necessarily best quality. It is determined by the cost of the product and the technical characteristics as suited to the specific requirements.

2. RIGHT QUANTITY

- The manufacturing organization should produce the products in right number.

- If they are produced in excess of demand the capital will block up in the form of inventory and if the quantity is produced in short of demand, leads to shortage of products.

3. RIGHT TIME

- Timeliness of delivery is one of the important parameter to judge the effectiveness of production department.

- So, the production department has to make the optimal utilization of input resources to achieve its objective.

4. RIGHT MANUFACTURING COST

- Manufacturing costs are established before the product is actually manufactured.

- Hence, all attempts should be made to produce the products at pre-established cost, so as to reduce the variation between actual and the standard (pre-established) cost.

OPERATING SYSTEM

- Operating system converts inputs in order to provide outputs which are required by a customer.

- It converts physical resources into outputs, the function of which is to satisfy customer wants *i.e.,* to provide some utility for the customer.

- In some of the organization the product is a physical good (hotels) while in others it is a service (hospitals). **Bus and taxi services, tailors, hospital and builders are the examples of an operating system.**

- ***Everett E. Adam & Ronald J. Ebert*** define operating system as, *"An operating system (function) of an organization is the part of an organization that produces the organization's physical goods and services."*

- ***Ray Wild*** defines operating system as, *"An operating system is a configuration of resources combined for the provision of goods or services."*

CONCEPT OF OPERATIONS

- An operation is defined in terms of the mission it serves for the organization, technology it employs and the human and managerial processes it involves.

- Operations in an organization can be categorized into manufacturing operations and service operations.

- Manufacturing operations is a conversion process that includes manufacturing yields a tangible output: a product, whereas, a conversion process that includes service yields an intangible output: a deed, a performance, an effort.

DISTINCTION BETWEEN MANUFACTURING OPERATIONS AND SERVICE OPERATIONS

Following characteristics can be considered for **distinguishing manufacturing operations with service operations:**

1. **Tangible/Intangible nature of output**
2. **Consumption of output**
3. **Nature of work (job)**
4. **Degree of customer contact**
5. **Customer participation in conversion**
6. **Measurement of performance.**

Manufacturing is characterized by
- tangible outputs (products),
- outputs that customers consume overtime,
- jobs that use less labour and more equipment,
- little customer contact,
- no customer participation in the conversion process (in production), and sophisticated methods for measuring

production activities and resource consumption as product are made.

Service is characterized by

- intangible outputs,
- outputs that customers consumes immediately,
- jobs that use more labour and less equipment,
- direct consumer contact,
- frequent customer participation in the conversion process,
- Elementary methods for measuring conversion activities and resource consumption.

Some services are equipment based namely rail-road services, telephone services and some are people based namely tax consultant services, hair styling.

OPERATIONS MANAGEMENT

A FRAMEWORK FOR MANAGING OPERATIONS

Managing operations can be enclosed in a frame of general management function.

Operation managers are concerned with planning, organizing, and controlling the activities which affect human behaviour through models.

PLANNING

- ***Activities that establishes a course of action and guide future decision-making is planning.***
- The operations manager defines the objectives for the operations subsystem of the organization, and the policies, and procedures for achieving the objectives.
- This stage includes clarifying the role and focus of operations in the organization's overall strategy.
- It also involves product planning, facility designing and using the conversion process.

ORGANIZING

- ***Activities that establishes a structure of tasks and authority.***
- Operation managers establish a structure of roles and the flow of information within the operations subsystem.

- They determine the activities required to achieve the goals and assign authority and responsibility for carrying them out.

CONTROLLING
- ***Activities that assure the actual performance in accordance with planned performance.***
- To ensure that the plans for the operations subsystems are accomplished, the operations manager must exercise control by measuring actual outputs and comparing them to planned operations management.
- Controlling costs, quality, and schedules are the important functions here.

BEHAVIOUR
- Operation managers are concerned with how their efforts to plan, organize, and control affect human behaviour.
- They also want to know how the behaviour of subordinates can affect management's planning, organizing, and controlling actions. Their interest lies in decision-making behaviour.

MODELS
- As operation managers plan, organize, and control the conversion process, they encounter many problems and must make many decisions.
- They can simplify their difficulties using models like *aggregate planning models* for examining how best to use existing capacity in short-term, *break even analysis* to identify break even volumes, *linear programming and computer simulation* for capacity utilisation, *decision tree analysis* for long-term capacity problem of facility expansion, *simple median model* for determining best locations of facilities etc.

SCOPE OF PRODUCTION AND OPERATIONS MANAGEMENT

- Production and operations management concern with the **conversion of inputs into outputs**, using physical resources, so as to provide the desired **utilities to the customer** while meeting the other organizational objectives of effectiveness, efficiency and adoptability.

- It distinguishes itself from other functions such as personnel, marketing, finance, etc., by its primary concern for **'conversion by using physical resources.'**

Following are the **activities which are listed under production and Operations management functions**:

1. **Location of facilities**
2. **Plant layouts and material handling**
3. **Product design**
4. **Process design**
5. **Production and planning control**
6. **Quality control**
7. **Materials management**
8. **Maintenance management.**

LOCATION OF FACILITIES

- Location of facilities for operations is a long-term capacity decision which involves a long term commitment about the geographically static factors that affect a business organization.
- It is an important strategic level decision-making for an organization. It deals with the questions such as 'where our main operations should be based?'
- The selection of location is a key-decision as large investment is made in building plant and machinery.
- An improper location of plant may lead to waste of all the investments made in plant and machinery equipments.
- Hence, location of plant should be based on the company's expansion plan and policy, diversification plan for the products, changing sources of raw materials and many other factors.
- The purpose of the location study is to find the optimal location that will results in the greatest advantage to the organization.

PLANT LAYOUT AND MATERIAL HANDLING

- Plant layout refers to the physical arrangement of facilities. It is the configuration of departments, work centres and equipment in the conversion process.
- The overall objective of the plant layout is to design a physical arrangement that meets the required output quality and quantity most
- economically.
- According to **James Moore,** *"Plant layout is a plan of an optimum arrangement of facilities including personnel, operating equipment, storage space, material handling equipments and all other supporting services along with the design of best structure to contain all these facilities".*
- 'Material Handling' refers to the 'moving of materials from the store room to the machine and from one machine to the next during the process of manufacture'.
- It is also defined as the 'art and science of moving, packing and storing of products in any form'.
- It is a specialized activity for a modern manufacturing concern, with 50 to 75% of the cost of production.
- This cost can be reduced by proper section, operation and maintenance of material handling devices.
- Material handling devices increases the output, improves quality, speeds up the deliveries and decreases the cost of production. Hence, material handling is a prime consideration in the designing new plant and several existing plants.

PRODUCT DESIGN

- Product design deals with conversion of ideas into reality. Every business organization have to design, develop and introduce new products as a survival and growth strategy.
- Developing the new products and launching them in the market is the biggest challenge faced by the organizations.

- The entire process of need identification to physical manufactures of product involves three functions: marketing, product development, manufacturing.
- Product development translates the needs of customers given by marketing into technical specifications and designing the various
features into the product to these specifications.
- Manufacturing has the responsibility of selecting the processes by which the product can be manufactured. Product design and development provides link between marketing, customer needs and expectations and the activities required to manufacture the product.

PROCESS DESIGN

- Process design is a macroscopic decision-making of an overall process route for converting the raw material into finished goods.
- These decisions encompass the selection of a process, choice of technology, process flow analysis and layout of the facilities.
- Hence, the important decisions in process design are to analyse the workflow for converting raw material into finished product and to select the workstation for each included in the workflow.

PRODUCTION PLANNING AND CONTROL

- Production planning and control can be defined as the process of planning the production in advance, setting the exact route of each item, fixing the starting and finishing dates for each item, to give production orders to shops and to follow up the progress of products according to orders.
- The principle of production planning and control lies in the statement 'First Plan Your Work and then Work on Your Plan'.
- Main functions of production planning and control includes planning, routing, scheduling, dispatching and follow-up.
- **Planning** is deciding in advance what to do, how to do it, when to do it and who is to do it.
- Planning bridges the gap from where we are, to where we want to go. It makes it possible for things to occur which would not otherwise happen.

- **Routing** may be defined as the selection of path which each part of the product will follow, which being transformed from raw material to finished products.
- Routing determines the most advantageous path to be followed from department to department and machine to machine till raw material gets its final shape.
- **Scheduling** determines the programme for the operations. Scheduling may be defined as 'the fixation of time and date for each operation' as well as it determines the sequence of operations to be followed.
- **Dispatching** is concerned with the starting the processes. It gives necessary authority so as to start a particular work, which has already been planned under 'Routing' and 'Scheduling'.
- Therefore, dispatching is 'release of orders and instruction for the starting of production for any item in acceptance with the route sheet and schedule charts'.
- The function of **follow-up** is to report daily the progress of work in each shop in a prescribed proforma and to investigate the causes of deviations from the planned performance.

QUALITY CONTROL

- Quality Control (QC) may be defined as 'a system that is used to maintain a desired level of quality in a product or service'.
- It is a systematic control of various factors that affect the quality of the product. Quality control aims at prevention of defects at the source, relies on effective feedback system and corrective action procedure.
- Quality control can also be defined as 'that industrial management technique by means of which product of uniform acceptable quality is manufactured'.
- It is the entire collection of activities which ensures that the operation will produce the optimum quality products at minimum cost.

The main objectives of quality control are:
- To improve the companies income by making the production more acceptable to the customers *i.e.*, by providing long life, greater usefulness, maintainability, etc.
- To reduce companies cost through reduction of losses due to defects.
- To achieve interchangeability of manufacture in large scale production.

- To produce optimal quality at reduced price.
- To ensure satisfaction of customers with productions or services or high quality level, to build customer goodwill, confidence and reputation of manufacturer.
- To make inspection prompt to ensure quality control.
- To check the variation during manufacturing.

MATERIALS MANAGEMENT

- Materials management is that aspect of management function which is primarily concerned with the acquisition, control and use of materials needed and flow of goods and services connected with the production process having some predetermined objectives in view.

The main objectives of materials management are:
- To minimise material cost.
- To purchase, receive, transport and store materials efficiently and to reduce the related cost.
- To cut down costs through simplification, standardisation, value analysis, import substitution, etc.
- To trace new sources of supply and to develop cordial relations with them in order to ensure continuous supply at reasonable rates.
- To reduce investment tied in the inventories for use in other productive purposes and to develop high inventory turnover ratios.

MAINTENANCE MANAGEMENT

- In modern industry, equipment and machinery are a very important part of the total productive effort.
- Therefore, their idleness or downtime becomes are very expensive. Hence, it is very important that the plant machinery should be properly maintained.

The main objectives of maintenance management are:
1. To achieve minimum breakdown and to keep the plant in good working condition at the lowest possible cost.

2. To keep the machines and other facilities in such a condition that permits them to be used at their optimal capacity without interruption.

3. To ensure the availability of the machines, buildings and services required by other sections of the factory for the performance of their functions at optimal return on investment.

BENEFITS DERIVED FROM EFFICIENT PRODUCTION MANAGEMENT

The efficient Production Management will give benefits to the **various sections of the society**. They are:

(*i*) **Consumer** benefits from improved industrial Productivity, increased use value in the product.

Products are available to him at right place, at right price, at right time, in desired quantity and of desired quality.

(*ii*) **Investors:** They get increased security for their investments, adequate market returns, and creditability and good image in the society.

(*iii*) **Employee** gets adequate Wages, Job security, improved working conditions and increased Personal and Job satisfaction.

(*iv*) **Suppliers:** Will get confidence in management and their bills can be realized without any delay.

(*v*) **Community:** community enjoys Benefits from economic and social stability.

(*vi*) **The Nation** will achieve prospects and security because of increased Productivity and healthy industrial atmosphere.

History of operations management

INTRODUCTION

- Production/operations management is the process, which combines and transforms various resources used in the production/operations subsystem of the organization into value added product/services in a controlled manner as per the policies of the organization.

- Therefore, it is that part of an organization, which is concerned with the transformation of a range of inputs into the required (products/serv ces) having the requisite quality level.

- The set of interrelated management activities, which are involved in **manufacturing** certain products, is called as **production management**.

- If the same concept is extended to **services** management, then the corresponding set of management activities is called as **operations management**.

HISTORICAL EVOLUTION OF PRODUCTION AND OPERATIONS MANAGEMENT

- For over two century's operations and production management has been recognized as an important factor in a country's economic growth.

- The traditional view of manufacturing management began in eighteenth century when **Adam Smith** recognized the economic benefits of specialization of labour.
- He recommended breaking of jobs down into subtasks and recognizes workers to specialized tasks in which they would become highly skilled and efficient.

- In the early twentieth century, **F.W. Taylor** implemented Smith's theories and developed scientific management.

- From then till **1930,** many techniques were developed prevailing the **traditional view.** Brief information about the **contributions to manufacturing management** is shown in the **Table.**

Historical summary of operations management

Date	Contribution	Contributor
1776	Specialization of labour in manufacturing	Adam Smith
1799	Interchangeable parts. cost accounting	Eli Whitney and others
1832	Division of labour by skill: assignment of jobs by skill: basics of time study	Charles Babbage
1900	Scientific management time study and work study developed: dividing planning and doing of work	Frederick W. Taylor
1900	Motion of study of jobs	Frank B. Gilbreth
1901	Scheduling techniques for employees. machines jobs in manufacturing	Henry L. Gantt
1915	Economic lot sizes for inventory control	F.W. Harris
1927	Human relations: the Hawthorne studies	Elton Mayo
1931	Statistical inference applied to product quality: quality control charts	W.A. Shewart
1935	Statistical sampling applied to quality control: inspection sampling plans	H.F. Dodge & H.G. Roming
1940	Operations research applications in World War II	P.M. Blacker and others.
1946	Digital computer	John Mauchlly and J.P. Eckert
1947	Linear programming	G.B. Dantzig. Williams & others
1950	Mathematical programming. on-linear and stochastic processes	A. Chames. W.W. Cooper & others
1951	Commercial digital computer: large-scale computations available.	Sperry Univac
1960	Organizational behaviour: continued study of people at work	L. Cummings. L. Porter
1970	Integrating operations into overall strategy and policy. Computer applications to manufacturing. Scheduling and control. Material requirement planning (MRP)	W. Skinner J. Orlicky and G. Wright
1980	Quality and productivity applications from Japan: robotics. CAD-CAM	W.E. Deming and J. Juran.

- **Production management** becomes the acceptable term from **1930s to 1950s.**

- As F.W. Taylor's works become more widely known, managers developed techniques that focused on economic efficiency in manufacturing.

- Workers were studied in great detail to eliminate wasteful efforts and achieve greater efficiency. At the same time, psychologists, socialists and other social scientists began to study people and human behaviour in the working environment.

- In addition, economists, mathematicians, and computer socialists contributed newer, more sophisticated analytical approaches.

- With the 1970s emerges two distinct changes in our views. The most obvious of these, reflected in the new name **operations management** was a shift in the service and manufacturing sectors of the economy.

- As service sector became more prominent, the change from 'production' to 'operations' emphasized the broadening of our field to service organizations.

- The second, more suitable change was the beginning of an emphasis on synthesis, rather than just analysis, in management practices.

PRODUCTION PROCESSES

BRIDGE (PRODUCTION PROCESSES)

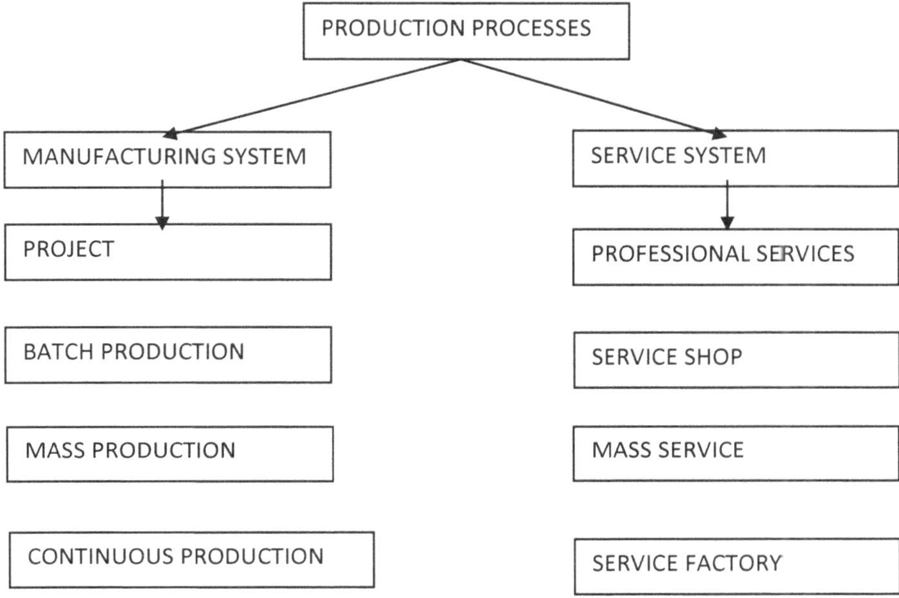

VARIOUS TYPES OF MANUFACTURING AND SERVICE SYSTEMS

1. Manufacturing systems

2. Service systems

Manufacturing systems

- **Project**

- **Batch production**

- **Mass production**

- **Continuous production**

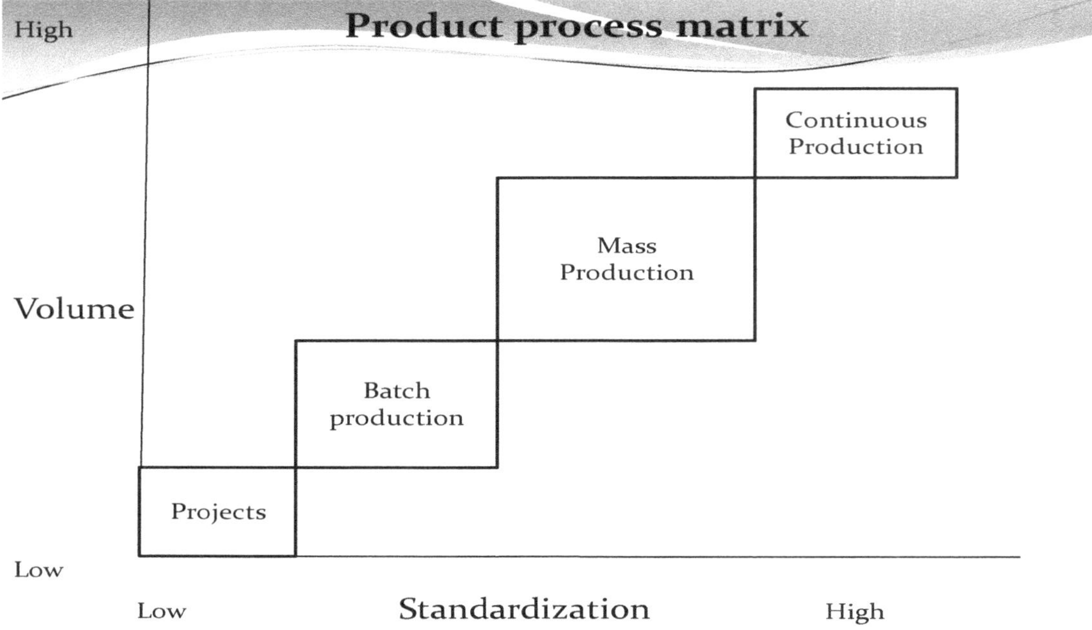

1. **Project**
   - Goods are produced according to orders and specifications
   - No continuous demands
   - Manufacturing is done when there are orders
   - Takes a long time to complete
   - Involves a large investment of funds
   - Produces one item at a time to customer order
   - **Eg.** – Construction projects, shipbuilding, aircraft manufacturing.

2. **Batch production**
   - Manufacturing is done in batches or groups.
   - Lots are either on the basis of customer specifications or with a hope of demand.
   - It processes many different jobs through the production system at the same time in groups or batches
   - Products are made to customers order

- Volume is low
- Demand fluctuates
- **Eg.** – medicines, furniture, bakeries

3. Mass production

- Produces large volumes of a standard product for a mass market.
- Demand is stable
- Volume is high
- **Eg.**- automobile, computers, most consumer goods

4. Continuous production

- Used for very high – volume commodity products that are very standardized.
- The system is highly automated
- In operation continuously for 24 hours a day
- **Eg.**- refined oil, paints, chemicals

SERVICE SYSTEMS

- **Professional services**
- **Service shop**
- **Mass services**
- **Service factory**

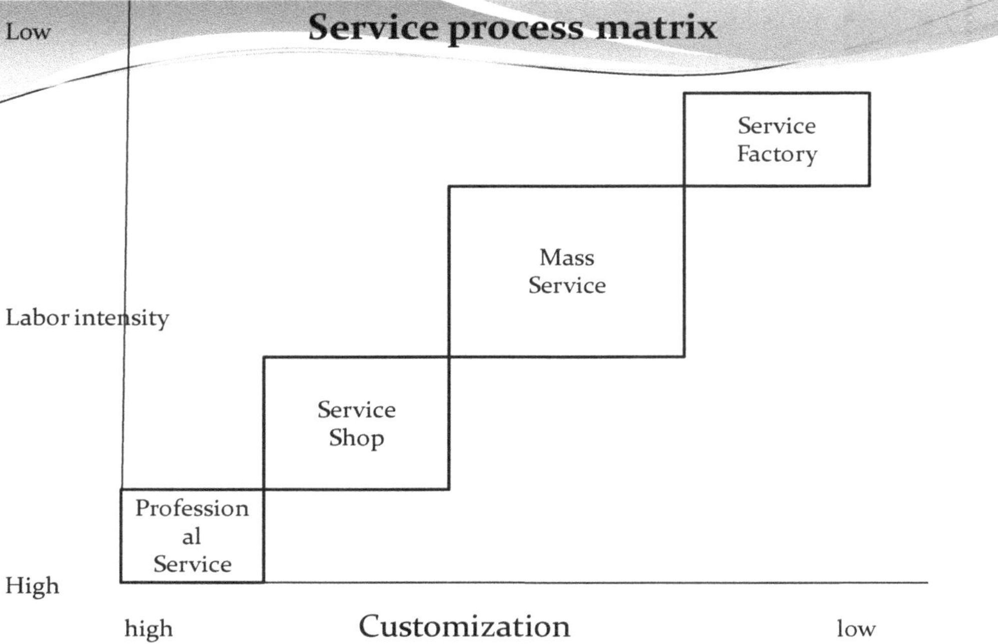

1. Professional services
- Highly customized, very labor intensive
- **Eg.**- accountants, lawyers, doctors

2. Service shop
- Less customized and less labor intensive but still attentive to individual customers
- **Eg.**- schools, hospitals

3. Mass services
- Offers same basic services to all customers and allows less interaction with service provider
- **Eg.**- retailing, banking

4. Service factory
- Services with least degree of customization and labor intensity
- **Eg.**- electricity, transportation

<u>PRODUCT DESIGN AND PROCESS SELECTION</u>

PRODUCT DESIGN

- A way for manufacturers to **satisfy customers** and **gain a differential advantage**.

- It refers to the arrangement of elements that collectively form a good or service.

- It is concerned with the form and function of a product.

- Form design involves the determination of **what a product would look like**,

  i.e. the shape and appearance of the product.

- It is concerned with **appearance and aesthetic considerations** and the **size**, **volume** and **weight** of the product which are generally secondary to the performance of the product.

- Functional design deals with what function the product will perform and how it performs.

- It is concerned with the first and foremost requirement of a good product.

  i.e. the product should effectively perform the function for which it is developed.

- **E.g.**- for a television set, the picture quality-video and the sound quality-audio is more important than the appearance of the cabinet in which the picture tube is fixed.

PROCESS DESIGN

- Is concerned with the overall **sequences of operations** required to achieve the design specification of the product.

- It specifies the type of **work stations** that are to be used, the machines and equipments necessary to carry out the processes to produce the product.

- The choice of process technology and process design is related to product design.

- Because manufacturing must be capable of achieving the product specified in the product design.

IMPORTANCE OF PRODUCT DESIGN

- As products are designed, all the detailed characteristics of each product are established.

- Each product characteristic directly affects **how the product can be made** or produced

  i.e.-process technology and process design

- How the product is made determines the design of production system-production design which is heart of production and operation strategy.

- Product design affects **product quality, production cost and customer satisfaction**.

- A good product design can improve the **marketability** of a product by

    - making it easier to operate or use

- upgrading its quality

- improving its appearance

- reducing manufacturing costs

- A distinctive design may be the only feature that significantly **differentiates** a product.

- An excellent design includes

- usability

- reliability

- functionality

- innovation

- appropriateness

FACTORS INFLUENCING PRODUCT DESIGN

- Customer requirements

- Convenience of the operator or user

- Trade off between function and form

- Types of material used

- Work methods and equipments

- Cost/price ratio

- Product quality

- Process capability

- Effect on existing products

- Packaging

CHARACTERISTICS OF GOOD PRODUCT DESIGN

- Function
- Appearance
- Reliability
- Maintainability
- Availability
- Producibility
- Simplification
- Standardization
- Specification
- Safety

THE DESIGN PROCESS

1. Idea generation
2. Feasibility study
3. Preliminary design
4. Form design
5. Functional design
6. Production design
7. Final design and process plans

<u>FACILITY LAYOUT</u>

BRIDGE

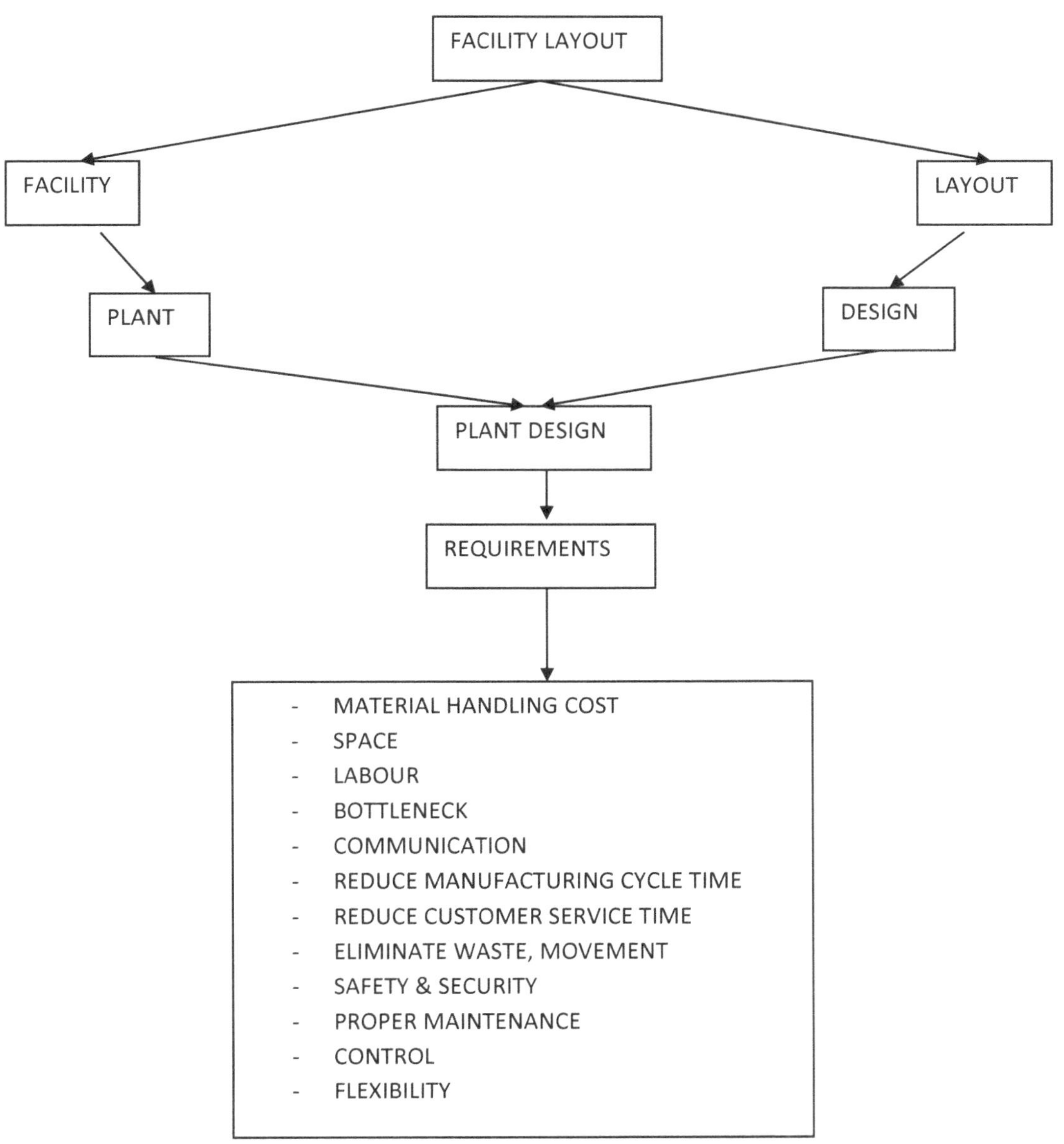

INTRODUCTION

- Layout decisions entail determining the placement of departments, work groups within the departments, workstations, machines, and stock-holding points within a production facility.

- The objective is to arrange these elements in a way that ensures a smooth work flow (in a factory) or a particular traffic pattern (in a service organization). In general, the inputs to the layout decision are as follows:

1 Specification of the objectives and corresponding criteria to be used to evaluate the design. The amount of space required, and the distance that must be traveled between elements in the layout, are common basic criteria.

2 Estimates of product or service demand on the system.

3 Processing requirements in terms of number of operations and amount of flow between the elements in the layout.

4 Space requirements for the elements in the layout.

5 Space availability within the facility itself, or if this is a new facility, possible building configurations.

OBJECTIVE

- Basic objective of layout is to ensure a smooth flow of work, material, and information through the system.

Requirements for effective layout

- Minimize material handling costs;
- Utilize space efficiently;
- Utilize labor efficiently;

- Eliminate bottlenecks
- Facilitate communication and interaction between workers, between workers and their supervisors, or between workers and customers
- Reduce manufacturing cycle time and customer service time
- Eliminate wasted or redundant movement
- Facilitate the entry, exit, and placement of material, products, and people
- Incorporate safety and security measures; Promote product and service quality
- Encourage proper maintenance activities
- Provide a visual control of operations or activities
- Provide flexibility to adapt to changing conditions

BASIC LAYOUTS

There are 3 basic types of layouts:

- **process**
- **product**
- **fixed - position**

There are 3 hybrid types of layouts

- **cellular**
- **flexible manufacturing systems**
- **mixed model assembly-lines**

1. **Process Layouts**

- Process layouts (also known as functional layouts)
- definition:

   " A layout that groups similar activities together in departments of work centers according to the process or function that they perform."

- characteristic of operations that serve different customers different needs
- The equipment in a process layout is general purpose
- Workers are skilled at operating the equipment in their department
- The advantage of process layout is flexibility

- The disadvantage is inefficiency
- Process layouts are inefficient because jobs or customers do not flow through in an orderly fashion; backtracking is common
- Plus the workers may experience much "idle time" if they are waiting for more work to arrive from a different department
- Material storage space in a process layout must be large to accommodate the large amount of in-process inventory
- This inventory is high because material moves from work-center to work-center waiting to be processed
- Finished goods inventory however is low because goods are being made for particular customers
- Process layouts in manufacturing firms require flexible material handling equipment (such as forklifts) that can follow multiple paths, move in any direction, and carry large loads of in-process goods
- All areas of the facility must have timely access to the material handling equipment
- Process layouts in service firms require large aisles for customers to move back and forth and ample display space to accommodate different customer preferences

2. Product Layout

- Product layouts (also known as assembly lines)
- definition:

"Product layouts arrange activities in a line according to the sequence of operations that need to be performed to assemble a particular product."

- Each Product should have its own "line"
- Product layouts are suitable for mass production or repetitive operations in which demand is steady and volume is high
- Because of this product layouts are more autonomous than process layouts
- The advantage of the product layout is its efficiency and ease of use
- The disadvantage is its inflexibility
- each product must have a completely different assembly-line set up
- The major concern in a product layout is balancing the assembly line so that no one workstation becomes a bottleneck and holds up the flow of work through the line

- A product layout needs material moved in one direction along the assembly line and always in the same pattern
- The most common material handling equipment used in product layouts is the convey or
- conveyors can be automatic (at a steady speed), or paced by the workers
- Aisles are narrow because material is moved only one way, it is not moved very far
- Scheduling of the conveyors, once they are installed, is simple--the only variable is how fast they should operate
- Storage space along an assembly line is quite small because in-process inventory is consumed in the assembly of the product as it moves down the assembly line
- Finished good inventory may require a separate warehouse for storage before they are sold

3. Fixed-Position Layouts

- Fixed-Position Layout
- definition: Fixed-Position layouts are layouts are used in projects in which the product is too fragile, bulky, or heavy to move
- examples: ships, houses, aircraft
- equipment, material, and workers are brought to the production site
- the equipment is often left on-site because it is too expensive to move frequently
- The workers on such job sites are highly skilled at performing the special tasks that they are requested to do
- In such a process the fixed costs would be low and variable costs would be high

4. Cellular Layouts

- Cellular layouts attempt to combine the flexibility of a process layout with the efficiency of a product layout
- Based on the concept of **group technology** (GT), dissimilar machines are grouped into work centers, called *cells,* to process parts with similar shapes or processing requirements
- The layout of machines *within* each cell resembles a small assembly line

- Production flow analysis (PFA) is a group technology technique that reorders part routing matrices to identify families of parts with similar processing requirements

Advantages of cellular layout

- Reduced material and Transit time
- Reduced Setup time
- Reduced work-in-process inventory
- Better use of human resources
- Easier to control

Disadvantages of a cellular layout

- Inadequate part families
- Poorly balanced cells
- Expanded training and scheduling of workers
- Increased capital investment
- Cellular layout have become popular in the past decade as the backbone of modern factories

5. Flexible Manufacturing Systems

- A flexible manufacturing system can produce an enormous variety of items
- An FMS is large, complex, and expensive
- The emphasis for FMS is on automation
- Computers run all the machines that complete the process
- Not many industries can afford traditional FMS hence the trend is towards smaller versions call flexible manufacturing cells

6. Mixed-Model Assembly Lines

- Some manufacturers changed their forecasting techniques to account for this
- The problem with the traditional layout is that it does take into account consumers change in demand
- Others adopted a mixed-model assembly line technique instead

There are several steps involved in a mixed-model assembly

- The first step is to reduce the amount of time needed to change over the line to produce different models
- Then they trained their workers to perform a variety of tasks and allowed them to work at more than one workstation on the line
- Then the organization must change the way the line is arranged and scheduled
- There are also several factors to consider in designing a mixed-model assembly line

Line Balancing

U-shaped lines

Flexible workforce

Model sequencing

- **Line Balancing**

  In a mixed-model line, the time to complete a task can vary from model to model

  When planning the completion time an array of values is used

  Otherwise, mixed-model lines are balanced in much the same way as single-model lines

- **U-shaped lines**

  To compensate for the different work requirements of assembling different models, it is necessary to have a flexible workforce and to arrange the line so that workers can assist one another as needed

  Efficiency of the assembly line can be improved with a u-shaped line

- **Flexible workforce**

Although worker paths are predetermined to fit within a set cycle time, the use of average time values in mixed-model lines will produce variations in worker performance. Hence, the lines are not run at a set speed. Items move through the line at the pace of the slowest operation

- **Model Sequencing**

  Since different models are produced on the same line, mixed-model scheduling involves an additional decision--the order, or sequence, of models to be run through the line

  Another objective in model sequencing is to spread out the production of different models as evenly as possible throughout the time period scheduled

<u>FACILITY LOCATION</u>

BRIDGE

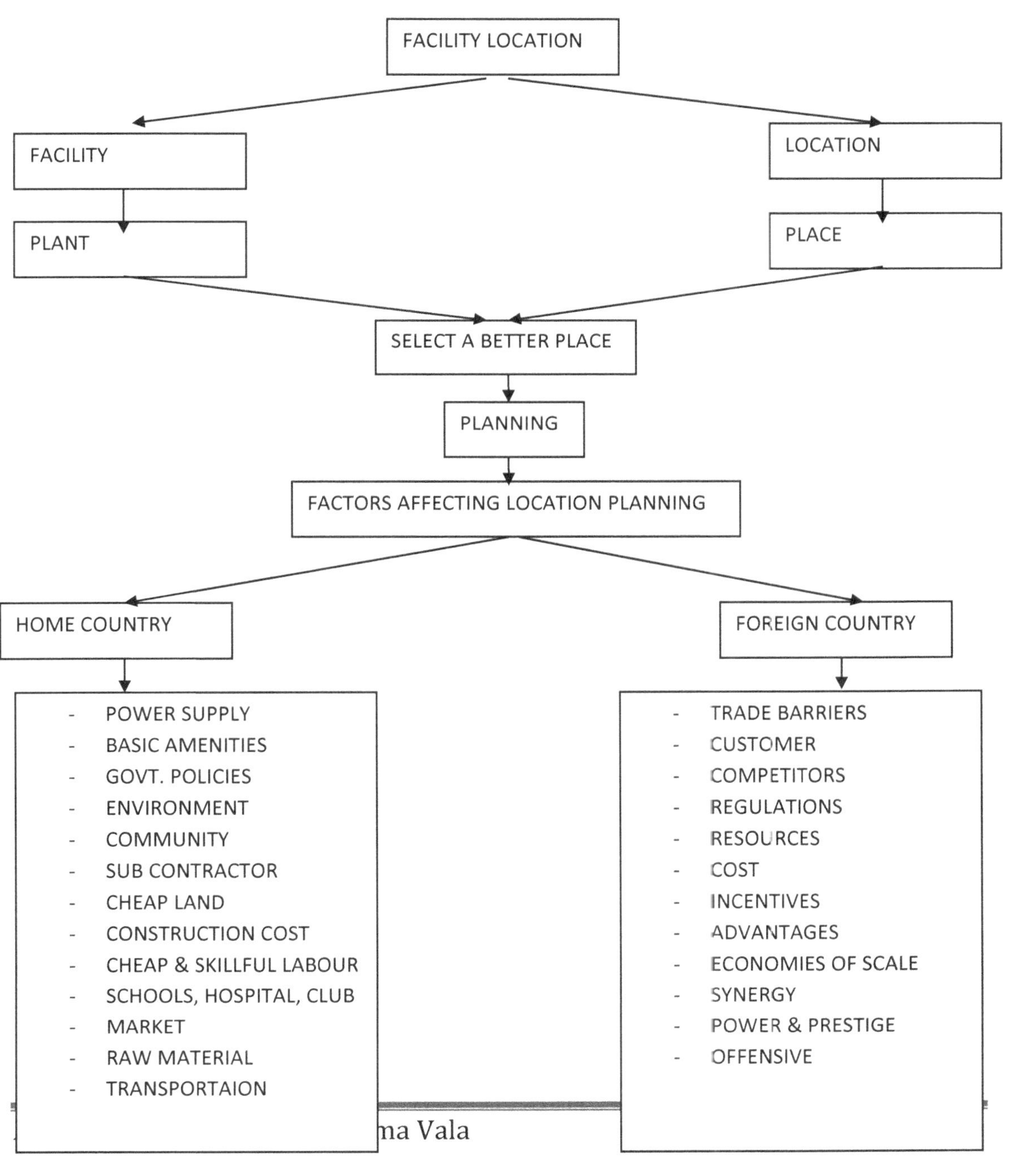

ma Vala

What does Facility location mean?

Facility location is actually a term used in operation management, facility location or location analysis is done so that the **better uses of the location** can be understood.

The company by understanding the materials and production process done nearby the location can save ample time in production process and also save a lot in terms of transportation cost.

And also the company can find out optimum position for the location of the company so that all the factors that are needed will be not a long distance from the company.

Some of the benefits in location analysis include:

- You get a thorough knowledge of all the factors involved in the production, and ways through which the materials that are needed in the production can easily be accessed.

- When you do a proper location analysis for your facility you will also come across alternate substitute materials that are readily available and will cost less.

- You can save a lot on transportation cost for materials, labour, import and export.

- The materials will be available at a comparatively low cost.

- The best way to get a task done is by finding out ways through which the task can be done. Location analysis helps you in those aspects.

- Allows to you differentiate between practical positions to place your facility. Like for example, you cannot build a hazardous facility in a residential area.

- Gives you access to cheap labour, and needed raw materials like water electricity and many more.

- Helps in a smooth running of an organization, by seeing to that all that is possibly needed is readily and easily available.

- Also has very easy access to production, distribution and sale of the products.

- Allows you to outperform your competitor's facilities

Once you have found the optimal location then you will very easily overcome all the issues that you are likely to face and have a smooth running of an organization. When you plan accordingly, you will also be prepared to face some minor hindrances.

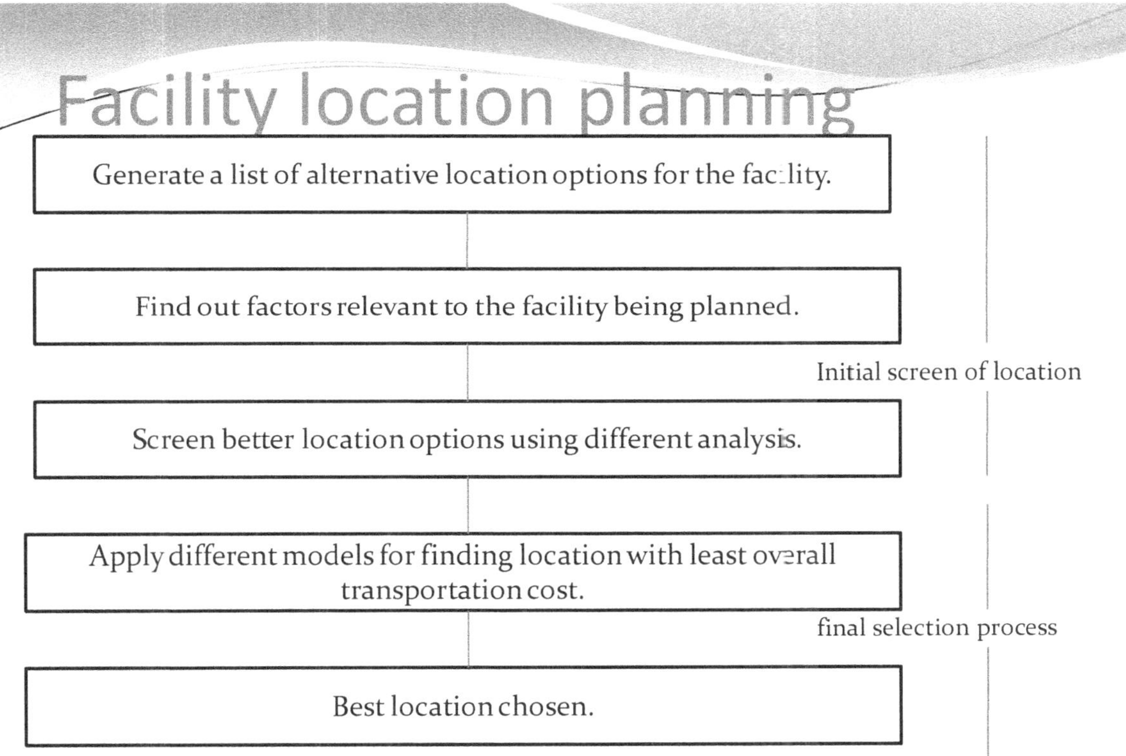

Factors Affecting Facility Location Planning

- Availability of power supply

- Basic amenities

- Government policies

- Environment & community

- Proximity to subcontractor

- Easy availability of cheap land

- Low construction cost

- Availability of cheap and skillful labour

- Residential complexes, schools, hospitals, clubs, etc.

- Proximity to markets

- Proximity to raw material

- Good transportation facilities

Locating Foreign Operations Facilities

- Trade barriers

- International customers

- International competition

- Regulations

- Additional resources

- Low cost

- Incentives

- Exploitation of firm specific advantages

- Economies of scale

- Synergy

- Power and prestige

- Offensive in competitor's home country

ASSEMBLY- LINE BALANCING

- Though primarily a scheduling issue, assembly-line balancing often has implications for layout.
- This would occur when, for balance purposes, workstation size or the number used would have to be physically modified.
- The most common assembly line is a moving conveyor that passes a series of work stations in a uniform time interval called the **workstation cycle time** (which is also the time between successive units coming off the end of the line).
- At each work station, work is performed on a product either by adding parts or by completing assembly operations.
- The work performed at each station is made up of many bits of work, termed *tasks, elements,* and *work units*.
- Such tasks are described by motion–time analysis.
- Generally, they are groupings that cannot be subdivided on the assembly line without paying a penalty in extra motions.
- The total work to be performed at a workstation is equal to the sum of the tasks assigned to that workstation.
- The **assembly-line balancing** problem is one of assigning all tasks to a series of workstations so that each workstation has no more than can be done in the work station cycle time, and so that the unassigned (that is, idle) time across all workstations is minimized.
- The problem is complicated by the relationships among tasks imposed by product design and process technologies.
- This is called the **precedence relationship,** which specifies the order in which tasks must be performed in the assembly process.

The steps in balancing an assembly line are straight forward:

1 Specify the sequential relationships among tasks using a precedence diagram. The diagram consists of circles and arrows. **Circles represent individual tasks; arrows indicate the order of task performance.**

2 Determine the required workstation cycle time (*C*), using the formula
C = Production time per day / Required output per day *(in units)*

3 Determine the theoretical minimum number of workstations (*Nt*) required to satisfy the workstation cycle time constraint using the formula (note that this must be rounded up to the next highest integer).
Nt = Sum of task times *(T) /* Cycle time *(C)*

4 Select a primary rule by which tasks are to be assigned to workstations, and a secondary rule to break ties.

5 Assign tasks, one at a time, to the first workstation until the sum of the task times is equal to the workstation cycle time, or no other tasks are feasible because of time or sequence restrictions. Repeat the process forWorkstation 2,Workstation 3, and so on until all tasks are assigned.

6 Evaluate the efficiency of the balance derived using the formula4
Efficiency = Sum of task times *(T)/*Actual number of workstations *(Na)* ×Workstation cycle time *(C)*

7 If efficiency is unsatisfactory, rebalance using a different decision rule.

AGGREGATE PLANNING

INTRODUCTION

Organizations make supply and capacity decisions on three levels:

1. Long term: Product and service selection, facility size and location, equipment, and facility layout.
2. Intermediate term: Employment, output, and inventory.
3. Short term: Scheduling of jobs, workers and equipment, and the like.

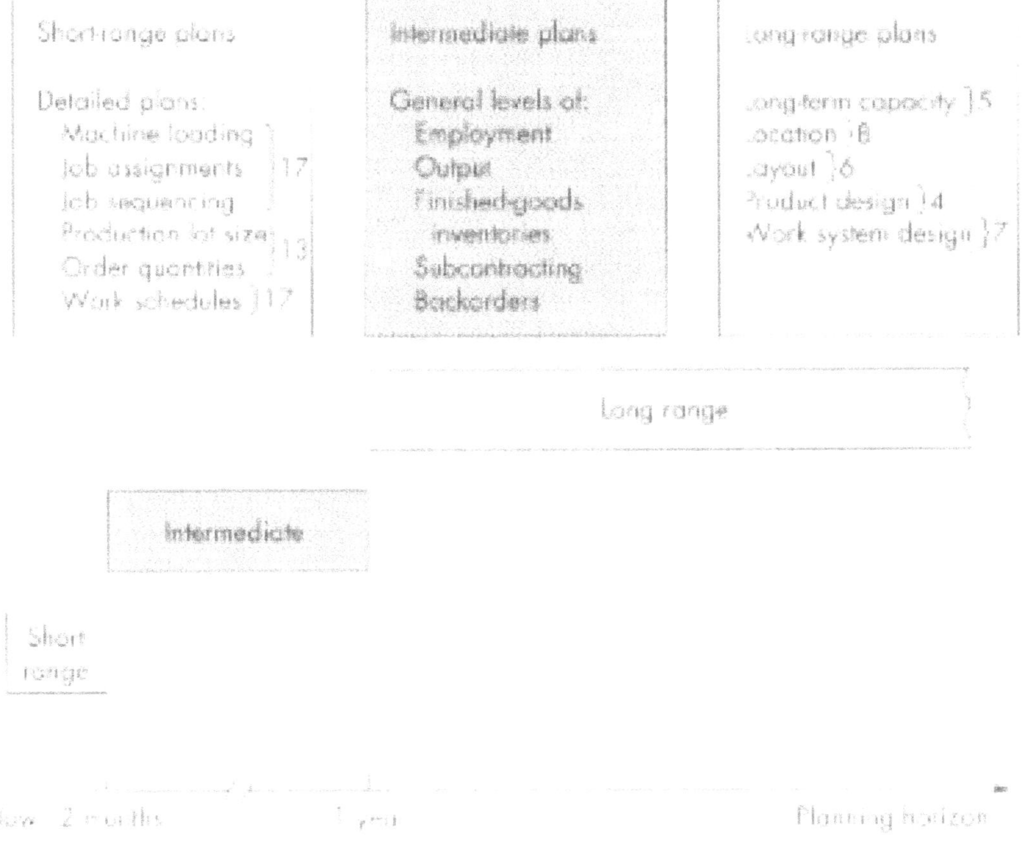

- Intermediate-range planning or aggregate/production planning balances supply and demand by minimizing the production cost, adjustment cost, and opportunity cost of a system.
- Planners are concerned with the quantity and the timing of both the supply and demand. Special challenge comes from uneven demand within the planning horizon.
- For example, in a department store, space allocation is often an aggregate decision. That is, the manager might decide to allocate 20 percent of the available space in the clothing department to women's sportswear, 30 percent to juniors, and so on, without regard for what brand names will be offered or how much of juniors will be slacks.
- The aggregate measure might be square feet of space or racks of clothing. The allocation might change over time.
- Aggregate planning typically covers a time horizon of 2 to 18 months, i.e., a *rolling planning horizon* covering the next 2-18 months. It is essentially a "big picture" approach to planning.
- Planners focus on a group of similar products or services, or sometimes an entire product or service line.
- The aggregate planning is particularly useful for organizations that experience seasonal or other fluctuations in demand or capacity.
- Two major reasons of doing intermediate-range planning are *time* and *level of accuracy*.
- It takes time to develop and implement a plan. It is also not possible to predict the timing and volume of demand for individual items with any degree of accuracy.
- The goal is to achieve a production plan that will effectively utilize an organization's resources to meet expected (forecasted) demand.
- Planners must make decisions on output rates, employment levels and changes, inventory levels and changes, back orders, and subcontracting.
- Inputs to aggregate planning include demand forecast, available resources, policies regarding employment levels, and so on.
- The output of the aggregate planning is a *production plan* or an *operations plan* with overall decisions on level of output, capacity, employment, and inventory.

Inputs	Outputs

Resources
  Workforce/production rates
  Facilities and equipment
Demand forecast
Policy statements on workforce changes
Subcontracting
Overtime
Inventory levels/changes
Back orders
Costs
  Inventory carrying cost
  Back orders
  Hiring/firing
  Overtime
  Inventory changes
  Subcontracting
	Total cost of a plan
	Projected levels of
	  Inventory
	  Output
	  Employment
	  Subcontracting
	  Backordering

DEMAND AND SUPPLY/CAPACITY OPTIONS

There are some decision options which planners can consider during aggregate planning.

DEMAND OPTIONS

Demand options can shift demand from peak periods to off-peak periods or create demand during off-peak periods so that the overall demand corresponds more closely to capacity in the planning horizon.

1. Pricing: An important factor to consider is *the degree of price elasticity*; the more the elasticity, the more effective pricing will be in influencing demand patterns.

Opportunity cost includes the lost profit stemming from capacity insufficient to meet demand during certain periods and the lost profit of lost demand due to the shift.

Examples of pricing are: low rates for weekend stay in a hotel, low fares for night travel of an airline, "early bird special" from a restaurant, and reduced matinee rates offered by a movie theater.

2. Promotion: The timing of promotion efforts and knowledge of response rates and response patterns will be needed to achieve the desired results.

   Unlike pricing, there is much less control over the timing of demand but more impact on quantity of the promoted products / services and the sales of their associated ones.

   There is always the risk that promotion can worsen the condition it was intended to improve.

3. Back orders: Back orders allow orders to be taken in one period and deliveries promised for a later period.

   The success of this approach depends on how willing customers are to wait for delivery.

   The costs associated with back orders are difficult to pin down and include lost sales, annoyed or disappointed customers, and perhaps additional paperwork.

4. New demand: Developing a demand for a complementary product (e.g., lawn mowers, garden equipment) that makes use of the same production processes achieves a more consistent use of labor, equipment, and facilities.

   Examples are: Creating new demand for buses at other times (e.g., trips by schools, clubs, and senior citizen groups) would make use of the excess capacity during those slack times; Opening fast food restaurants for breakfast to use their capacities more fully; Using landscaping equipment during the winter months for snow removal.

SUPPLY/CAPACITY OPTIONS

Capacity options allow planners to change supply by adjusting labor, inventory, and subcontracting.

- **Hire and lay off workers**: The extent to which operations are labor intensive determines the impact that changes in the workforce level will have on capacity.

  Of the cost involved in this option, hiring cost includes recruitment, screening, and training to bring new workers "up to speed." And, quality may suffer.

  Some savings may occur if workers who have recently been laid off are rehired. Layoff costs include severance pay, the cost of realigning the remaining workforce, potential bad feelings toward the firm on the part of workers who have been laid off, and some loss of morale for workers who are retained (i.e., in spite of company assurance, some workers will believe that in time they too may be laid off).

  In addition, other factors having impacts on this option include the availability of (in particular, skilled) workers and the contracts of unions.

- **Overtime / slack time**: The use of overtime can be especially attractive in dealing seasonal demand peaks by reducing the need to hire and train people who will have to be laid off during the off-season.

  Moreover, in situations with crews, it is often necessary to use a full crew rather than to hire one or two additional people. It should be noted that some union contractors allow workers to refuse overtime.

  Some people may not appreciate having to work on short notice or the fluctuations in income. Overtime could also result in lower productivity, poor quality, more accidents, and increased payroll costs.

  Slack time can result in less efficient use of machines and other fixed assets. Some organizations use slack time for training.

It also gives workers time for problem solving and process improvement, while retaining skilled workers.

- **Part-time workers**: The use of part-time workers depends on the nature of the work, training and skills needed, and union agreements.

  It costs less than regular workers in hourly wages and fringe benefits. Unions may regard such workers unfavorably because they typically do not pay union dues and may lessen the power of unions.

  Contract workers, also called independent contractors, have different pay scales and no benefits. They can be added or subtracted from the workforce with greater ease than regular workers, giving companies greater flexibility in adjusting the size of workforce.

- **Inventories**: Inventory can be built up during periods when production capacity exceeds demand and drawn down in periods when demand exceeds capacity.

  Inventory involves holding or carrying those goods as inventory until they are needed. The cost is tied up that could be invested elsewhere.

  Additional cost includes insurance, obsolescence, deterioration, spoilage, breakage, and so on.

  Although services tend not to make use of inventories to alter capacity requirements, a portion of the services can be done during slack periods (e.g., organize the workplace).

- **Subcontracting**: Subtracting enables planners to acquire temporary capacity with great flexibility.

  Factors to consider include availability capacity, relative expertise, quality considerations, cost, and the amount and stability of demand.

  As an alternative to subcontracting, an organization might consider outsourcing: contracting with another organization to supply some portion of the goods or services on a regular basis.

AGGREGATE PLANNING

- Aggregate planning is intermediate-range capacity planning used to establish employment levels, output rates, inventory levels, subcontracting, and backorders for products that are aggregated, i.e., grouped or brought together.
- It does not specifically focus on individual products but deals with the products in the aggregate.
- For example, imagine a paint company that produces blue, brown, and pink paints; the aggregate plan in this case would be expressed as the total amount of the paint without specifying how much of it would be blue, brown or pink.
- Such an aggregate plan may dictate, for example, the production of 100,000 gallons of paint during an intermediate-range planning horizon, say during the whole year.
- The plan can later be disaggregated as to how much blue, brown, or pink paint to produce every specific time period, say every month.
- Achieving a balance of expected supply and demand is the goal of aggregate planning.
- Informal graphical techniques, as well as mathematical techniques are used by decision makers to handle aggregate planning.

INFORMAL TECHNIQUES

Planners often use graphs or tables to compare current capacity with projected demand requirements.

The informal techniques provide some general information and insight but not the specific aggregate production details.

The graphs below depict aggregate planning using Level and Chase Strategies.

LEVEL STRATEGY

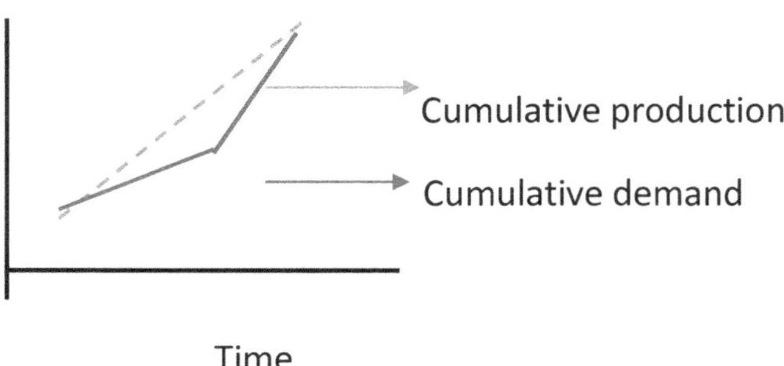

CHASE STRATEGY

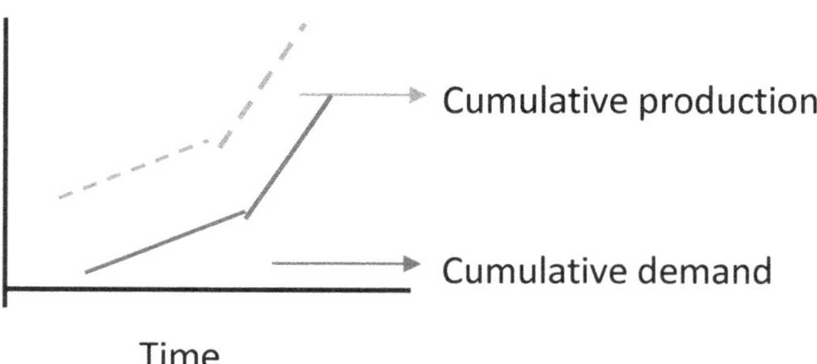

- In case of Level Strategy, production is uniform whereas in case of Chase Strategy, production chases the demand by fluctuating the work-force or work-force utilization.

- Organizations must compare work-force fluctuation costs with inventory costs to decide which strategy to use.
- Level Strategy is used when inventory costs are low as compared to the costs of fluctuating the work force and when efficient production is the primary goal.
- When inventory costs are high as compared to work force fluctuation costs, Chase Strategy is used, although it is less efficient for production.

AGGREGATE PLANNING STRATEGIES

Apart form the production strategies such as Level and Chase Strategies, we also have planning strategies.

There are three major strategies associated with aggregate planning:

1) product variations due to hiring, firing, overtime, or undertime,

2) permitting inventory levels to vary, and

3) subcontracting

An example depicting these strategies is presented below along with some sample computations of the costs associated with these strategies:

Level production is 300. Backorders are permitted. Initial Inventory is 70 units. 200 units are to be subcontracted for Period 6. Costs are as follows:

Product Variations	Inventory	Subcontracting	Shortage
$20 /unit	$3 /unit/period	$25 /unit	$7 /unit/period

PERIOD	DEMAND	PRODUCTION			INVENTORY				
		REGULAR	OVER	UNDER	BEG	END.	AVG.	SUB-CONTRACT	SHORTAGE
1	350	200	-	100	70	0	35	-	80
2	300	250	-	50	0	0	0	-	130
3	250	250	-	50	0	0	0	-	130
4	250	400	100	-	0	20	10	-	0
5	350	150	-	150	20	0	10	-	180
6	300	350	50	-	0	70	35	200	0
			500				90	200	520

Costs For The Above Plan:

Product Variations . . . . 500 x $20 = $10,000

Inventory. . . . . …… 90 x $ 3 = $ 270

Subcontracting . . . . 200 x $25 = $ 5,000

Shortage . . . . ……520 x $ 7 = $ 3,640

Total . . . . ……………. $18,910

ROUGH-CUT CAPACITY PLANNING

- Aggregate planning is based on a general production plan that deals with how much capacity will be available and how it will be allocated.
- A rough-cut capacity plan can be developed to evaluate the work load that a production plan imposes on work centers.
- Although a trial production plan is often used for rough-cut capacity planning, a trial master production schedule can be used too.
- The example below shows the application of rough-cut capacity planning based on a trial master schedule.

MASTER PRODUCTION SCHEDULE						
	MONTH					
PRODUCT	1	2	3	4	5	6
A	180	240	300	420	350	260
B	210	220	240	230	220	200
C	500	480	450	440	420	400
D	310	330	380	410	480	500

Below is a bill of labor which lists the hours   required in each department to make one unit of product.

PRODUCT				
DEPARMENT	A	B	C	D
11	0.4	0.2	0.7	0.5
22	0.1	0.6	0.4	0.9
33	1.1	0.3	0.7	0.6
44	0.3	0.8	0.2	0.5
55	0.5	0.0	0.4	0.6

Develop capacity requirements for the following combinations:

MONTH	DEPARTMENT
2	33
4	11
6	55
3	22

The solution is outlined below:

a. 240(1.1) + 220(0.3) + 480(0.7) + 330(0.6) = 864 hours

b. 420(0.4) + 230(0.2) + 440(0.7) + 410(0.5) = 727 hours

c. 260(0.5) + 200(0.0) + 400(0.4) + 500(0.6) = 590 hours

d. 300(0.1) + 240(0.6) + 450(0.4) + 380(0.9) = 696 hours

For example, we must have at least 864 hours available in Department 33 for Month 2 to meet capacity requirements. Suppose that we only have 640 man hours available in Department 33 in Month 2.

Then, we can use aggregate planning strategies such as hiring, overtime, etc. to bring the capacity up to the required amount of 864 man or machine hours in order to comply with master production schedule.

Note that this 864 hours is greater than the actual number of hours in a month(24 hours /day x 30 days / month = 720 hours / month).

We may encounter this situation often because we are talking about the man or machine hours.

For example, in case of a one 8-hour shift, 20 working days per month, and 10 workers, the man hours = 8 x 20 x 10 = 1,600.

WORK FORCE SIZE PLANNING

- In aggregate planning the major objective is to determine feasible and possibly optimal production quantities and the corresponding capacity (work force size) to accommodate such production requirements.
- An example of determining the appropriate work force size follows.
- The table below gives forecasted demand in four quarterly (3-month) periods:

Forecast Demand

Quarter	(standard units of work)
1	6,000
2	4,500
3	4,200
4	5,500
1 year	20,200

a. Assume employees contribute 180 regular working hours each month, and each unit requires 2 hours to produce. How many employees will be needed during Quarter 1 and Quarter 2?

b. What will be the average labor cost for each unit if the company pays employees $10/hour and maintains for the entire year a sufficient staff to meet the peak demand?

c. What percentage above the standard-hour cost is the company's average labor cost per unit in this year due to excess staffing for all but the peak quarterly period?

The solution is as follows:

a. Quarter 1:   6000 x 2 = 12,000 hours

12,000 / ▯ (180 x 3 months) = 22.22 ---> 23 employees

Quarter 2:   4,500 x 2 = 9,000

9,000 ▯/ (180 x 3 months) = 16.66 ---> 17 employees

b.   180 hours/employ.-month x 12 months x 23 employ. x \$10/hour   =

496,800/ 20,200 total units

= \$24.59/unit

c. 2 hours x \$10/hour = \$20/unit (standard cost)

\$24.59 -\$20   = 0.23 or 23% higher

\$20

OTHER MATHEMATICAL TECHNIQUES

The mathematical techniques used for aggregate planning vary from computer search models to heuristic and mathematical programming models.

Six techniques are discussed below.

1. ***Linear Programming*** -- LP models can be used to minimize the sum of costs related to aggregate planning such as regular labor time, overtime, subcontracting, inventory, and backorder costs.

    The solution generated by LP models are optimal under the assumptions of linear programming.   A linear programming application is shown below:

Suppose that the costs associated with various capacity options are as shown in the table below:

CAPACITY	PERIOD 1	PERIOD 2	COST
REGULAR	200	180	\$20 /unit
OVERTIME	80	60	\$25 /unit
SUBCONTRACT	100	100	\$30 /unit
DEMEND	340	300	
INVENTORY			
HOLDING COST			\$3 /unit/period

Backorders are not permitted in this case.

Then, the linear programming formulation could be obtained as follows:

		PERIOD 1		PERIOD 2		SUPPLY
PERIOD 1	REGULAR	X_{111}	20	X_{112}	23	200
	OVERTIME	X_{211}	25	X_{212}	28	80
	SUBCONTRACT	X_{311}	30	X_{312}	33	100
PERIOD 2	REGULAR			X_{122}	20	180
	OVERTIME			X_{222}	25	60
	SUBCONTRACT			X_{322}	30	100
	DEMAND	340		300		

For example, for X_{312} the first subscript (3) stands for the type of capacity (i.e. subcontract). The middle subscript (1) stands for the supplying period or production period (i.e. period 1). The last subscript (2) stands for the receiving period or consumption period (i.e. period 2).

LP formulation for the problem above:

Min $20X_{111} + 23X_{112} + 25X_{211} + 28X_{212} + 30X_{311} + 33X_{312} + 20X_{122} + 25X_{222} + 30X_{322}$

$X_{111} + X_{112} \leq 200$

$X_{211} + X_{212} \leq 80$

$X_{311} + X_{312} \leq 100$

$X_{122} \leq 180$

$X_{222} \leq 60$

$X_{322} \leq 100$

$X_{111} + X_{211} + X_{311} = 340$

$X_{112} + X_{212} + X_{312} + X_{122} + X_{222} + X_{322} = 300$

The solution to this LP could be obtained by a software like LINDO (Linear Interactive Discrete Optimizer). The optimal values of the variables such as x_{111}, x_{112}, x_{211}, etc. would show how much regular capacity, overtime capacity, etc. to use in each time period in order to minimize the cost of the planned aggregate production.

2.   ***Goal Programming*** -- is a special form of linear programming. Ordinary LP has only one objective or goal; it is to minimize the cost or maximize the profit. On the other hand, goal programming is used to optimize multiple goals; it is also possible to attach a certain priority to each goal. Like LP, goal programming is also an optimization technique.

3.   ***Linear Decision Rule*** -- calculus based approach that derives two linear equations from a quadratic equation which is nonlinear. One of the linear equations is used to plan the production levels and the other linear equation is used to plan the work force size.

4.   ***Management Coefficients*** -- this heuristic model attempts to improve planning performance using multiple regression. Past managerial performance is used as a base to improve performance.

5.   ***Parametric Production Planning*** -- this technique helps planning the production levels and work force levels by using a heuristic search routine.

6.   ***Simulation Models*** -- Many real life situations are simulated . The computerized simulation models are tested under these simulated conditions to determine the aggregate planning parameters such as production levels and work force sizes.

<u>INVENTORY MANAGEMENT</u>

What do we mean by inventory?

- The chapter discusses inventory (we use the word interchangeably with the word **'stock'**) predominantly as accumulations of transformed input resource. In fact, usually as accumulations of material, parts or products.
- It does however mention the broader use of the word inventory or stock to denote the organisation's 'stock' of people, machines, and other assets.
- You often hear economists talking of a stock of resources in this way.
- From here on however we use the word exclusively to mean an accumulation of materials.

Stock is both good and bad

The problem with inventory management is that keeping stock has both advantages and disadvantages.

The advantages include,

- Inventory allows customers to be served quickly and conveniently (otherwise you would have to make everything as the customer requested it).
- Inventory can be used so a company can buy in bulk, which is usually cheaper.
- Inventory allows operations to meet unexpected surges in demand.
- Inventory is an insurance if there is an unexpected interruption in supply from outside the operation or within the operation.
- Inventory allows different parts of the operation to be 'decoupled'. This means that they can operate independently to suit their own constraints and convenience while the stock of items between them absorbs short-term differences between supply and demand. In many ways this is the most significant advantage of inventory.

The disadvantages of inventory include,

- It is expensive. Keeping inventory means the company has to fund the gap between paying for the stock to be produced and getting revenue in by selling it. This is known as working capital. There is also the cost of keeping the stock in warehouses or containers.
- Items can deteriorate while they are being kept. Clearly this is significant for the food industry whose products have a limited life. However, it is also an issue for any other company because stock could be accidentally damaged while it is being stored.
- Products can become obsolescent while they are being stored. Fashion may change or commercial rivals may introduce better products.
- Stock is confusing. Large piles of inventory around the place need to be managed. They need to be counted, looked after and so on.

The objectives of inventory planning and control

Generally the operations objectives of managing the company's inventories include the following.

- Quality – products need to be maintained in as good a condition as possible while they are being stored. For perishable products this means not storing them for very long.
- Speed – inventories must be in the right place to ensure fast response to customer requests.
- Dependability – the right stock must be in the right place at the right time to satisfy customer demand. There is no point having the wrong products in stock.
- Flexibility – stock should be managed to allow the operation to be flexible. For example, that may mean keeping sufficient stock to allow the operations processes to switch to producing something else and yet being able to satisfy customers during that period from existing stock levels.
- Cost – if possible the total cost of managing stock levels should be minimised. This is the objective of the various quantitative models covered in the chapter.

Stock sometimes has unexpected advantages

- In some organizations stock may increase in value while it is being kept.
- Similarly the computer monitors illustrated are increasing in value in so much as the ones which are likely to fail early in their life are being identified.
- They will therefore not be shipped to customers and fail in use, which could damage the company's reputation.
- Another example is where a company deliberately purchases more stock than it needs because it feels the availability of the material or the price of the material is likely to change.
- Of course this is risky. Many companies have suffered severely by speculative purchasing of this type to avoid price increases only to see the prices drop.

Objective and Importance of Inventory Control

- Inventory control now-a- days has become unavoidable in any manufacturing process.
- The basic managerial objectives of inventory control are two fold :
  1 to avoid over and under investment in inventories; and
  2 To the right quality of goods of right quantity at proper time and at reasonable price the objective and importance of inventory control may be discussed as

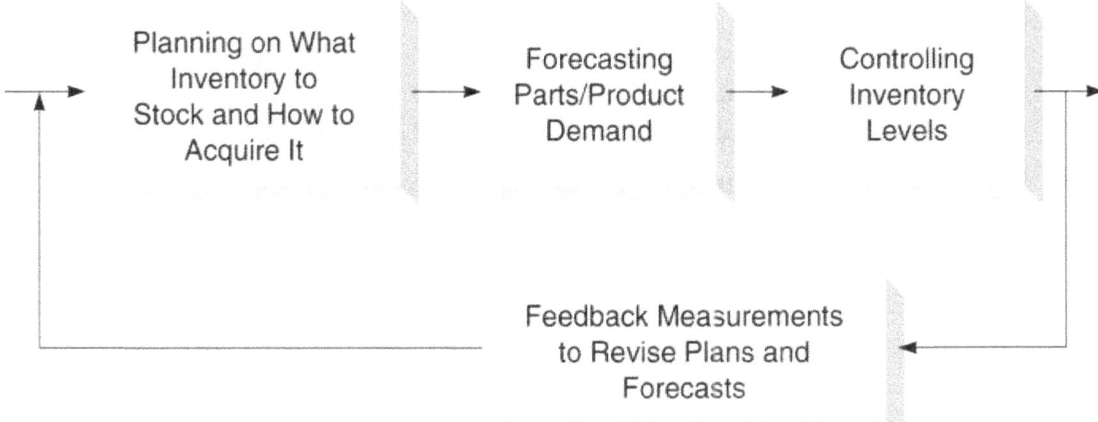

Fig. Inventory Planning Control

ASSUMPTION OF INVENTORY CONTROL

1. Demand is known and constant
2. Lead time is known and constant
3. Receipt of inventory is instantaneous
4. Quantity discounts are not available
5. Variable costs are limited to: ordering cost and carrying (or holding) cost
6. If orders are placed at the right time, stockouts can be avoided

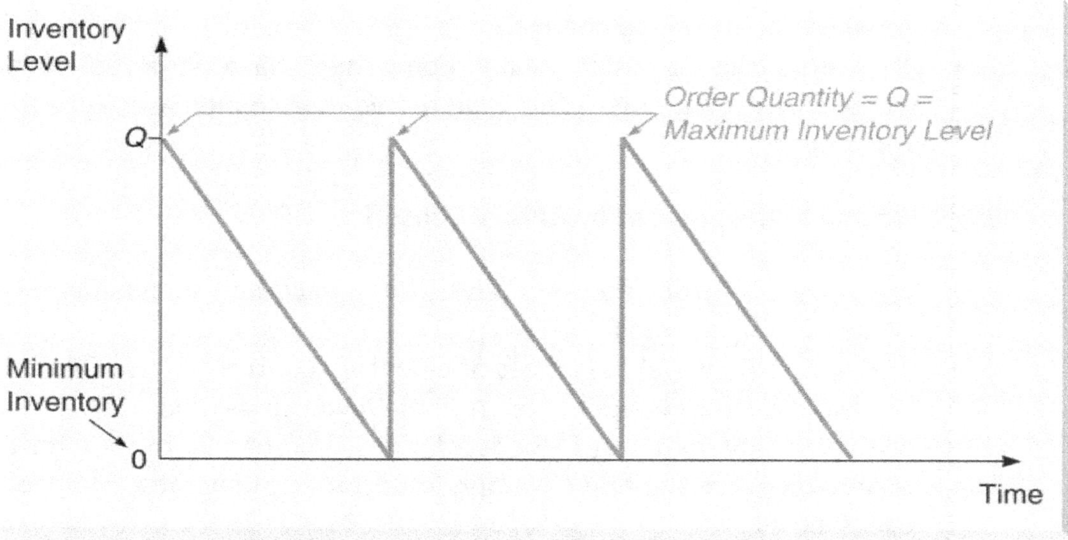

Fig.Inventory Level Overtime Based On Assumption.

MINIMIZE INVENTORY COST

- Only ordering and carrying costs need to be minimized (all other costs are assumed constant) As Q (order quantity) increases:
  1. Carry cost increases
  2. Ordering cost decreases (since the number of orders per year decreases)

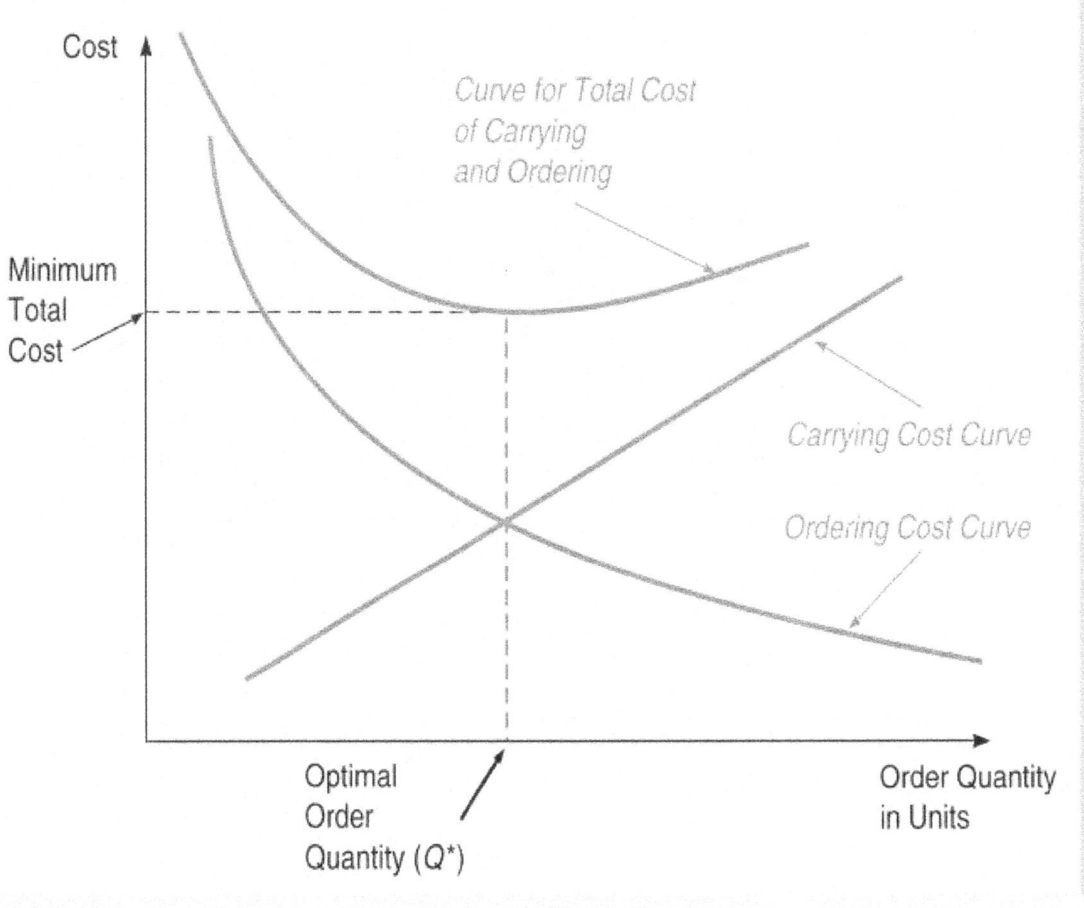

Fig .EOQ Model Total Cost. At optimal order quantity (Q*): Carrying cost = Ordering cost

ReorderPoint: Determining When to Order 1.After Q* is determined, the second decision is when to order 2.Orders must usually be placed *before* inventory reaches 0 due to order lead time 3.Lead time is the time from placing the order until it is received 4.The reorder point (ROP) depends on the lead time (L)

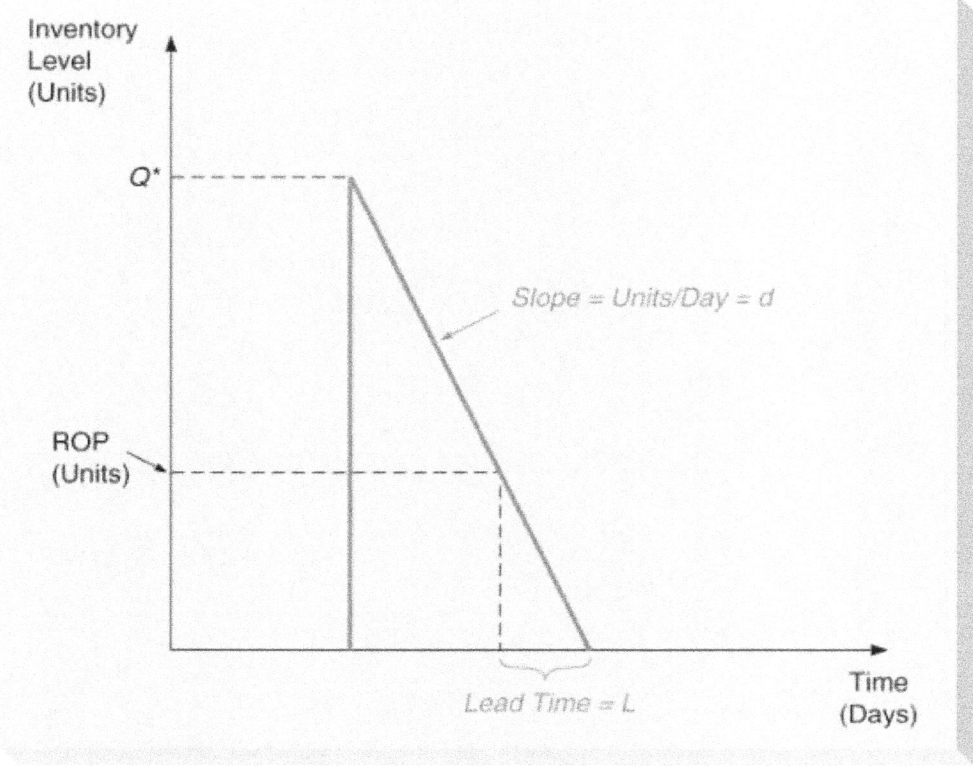

Fig. Reorder Point (ROP) ROP = d*L

Economic Production Quantity Determine How Much To Produce: 1.The EOQ model assumes inventory arrives Instantaneously. 2.In many cases inventory arrives gradually. 3.The **economic production quantity** (EPQ) model assumes inventory is being produced at a rate of p units per day. 4.There is a **setup cost** each time production begins..

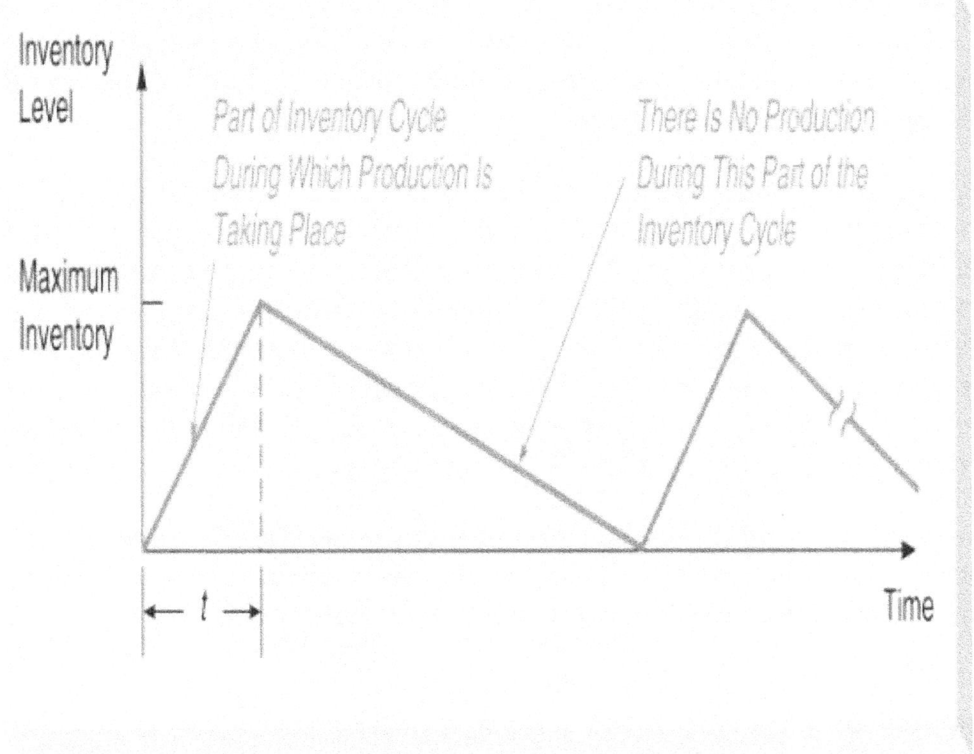

Fig .Inventory Control With Production.

INVENTORY CONTROL METHODS

Using the Item Warehouse Entry (IWE) screen, a warehouse manager specifies controls that help him or her to know when to reorder an item. Based on these controls, the NCAS notifies the warehouse manager when recorded inventory levels for an item fall below required levels. The NCAS uses one of the following inventory controls to calculate the reorder point for inventory items:

- **Order Point (O):** The **order point** is the quantity specified by the warehouse manager as the point at which the item should be reordered. If the available stock level reaches or falls below the order point quantity, the NCAS notifies the warehouse manager to reorder the item via the **Replenishment Action Report (RRACT).**

When the inventory control is O, the warehouse manager must also specify the quantity of stock to be reordered. The warehouse manager can use either a fixed order quantity or an economic order quantity to specify the quantity of stock to be reordered.

The **fixed order quantity** requires the warehouse manager to specify the amount of the item that should be ordered each time the available stock level falls to the order point. The fixed order quantity can be of two types: absolute or time supply. With the **absolute quantity**, the warehouse manager specifies a specific number of items to be ordered. With the **time supply quantity**, the order quantity is specified as a number of days' supply. If the order quantity is specified in days' supply, the NCAS calculates the quantity based upon the item's demand history.

If the warehouse manager selects the **economic (calculated) order quantity**, the NCAS calculates the optimal order quantity for the item based on minimizing the acquisition and carrying costs of the item.

- **Computed Order Point (C)**: The computed order point control is similar to the order point control. However, instead of using a fixed order point to determine when an item should be reordered, the NCAS uses the safety stock level, lead time, and forecasted monthly demand to calculate the order point. The **safety stock level** is the amount of cushion in units or in time for the item at the reorder point. The amount of cushion in time refers to the number of days that the current on-hand supply of an item will last. The **lead time** is the number of days from the time a purchase order is created until the goods are received at the warehouse.

  If the NCAS determines that an item with the computed order point control needs to be replenished, the item will appear on the **Replenishment Action Report** **(RRACT)**.

- **Minimum/Maximum (M)**: The minimum/maximum control specifies the point at which an item should be reordered (minimum stocking level) and a reorder quantity ceiling (maximum stocking level). The NCAS uses the order point (minimum stocking level), inventory standard (maximum stocking level), and order multiple to determine the order quantity.

- o When inventory levels for an item fall below the minimum, as designated by the value in the ORDER POINT field, the NCAS will notify the warehouse manager that replenishment should be initiated.
- o The **inventory standard** is the ceiling or maximum inventory level permitted for that item at that warehouse. In other words, replenishment should not exceed the inventory standard.
- o The **order multiple** is the multiple in which an order for an item should be placed. For example, a vendor only sells scissors by the dozen. Therefore, the buyer may only buy the scissors in multiples of 12. The buyer may buy 12, 24, 36, or 48 (and so on) pairs of scissors.

When the minimum/maximum control is selected, the NCAS does not allow an order that causes inventory to exceed the established inventory standard or maximum quantity. This is known as a maximum exception. In this case, the warehouse manager receives a warning message from the system. If this message is ignored, the order in question will be rerouted to a special warehouse approver to get approval to exceed the inventory standard.

In contrast, a minimum exception occurs when the inventory level of an item drops to or below the order point. When this occurs, the item will appear on the **Replenishment Action Report (RRACT)**. This report notifies the warehouse manager that it is time to replenish the item.

- **External (E)**: When the external control is utilized, the NCAS does not advise the warehouse manager when to initiate replenishment. The warehouse manager must complete this function manually. The warehouse manager may use some method external to the NCAS to determine when he or she should initiate replenishment of the item.

MATERIAL HANDLING

Material handling is an important element, which determines the productivity of a warehouse.

Material handling is highly labor intensive as compared to any other operations in a warehouse. Therefore the personnel cost in material handling is usually high.

Most of the activities in material handling require significant manual handling and hence has little benefits from computerization and improved information technology.

Objectives / Roles

1. Handling

The primary handling objective in a warehouse is to sort inbound shipment according to precise customer requirements. The three handling activities are receiving, in-storage handling and shipping.

2. Receiving:

When material reaches the warehouse it has to be received by the warehouse. One of the important activities here is to unload the goods from the transportation vehicle. Most of the time unloading is done manually. Containerized or unit-load shipments considerably reduce the unloading time.

3. In-storage Handling:

In-storage handling consists of all movement within a warehouse facility. The two types of in-storage handling are transfer and section.

Various transfers of goods happen within the warehouse. The goods as soon as they are received in the warehouse are transferred to the storage area.

The second transfer may be required during order selection where goods are transferred from storage area to order selection area. The final transfer of goods takes place when the goods are finally shipped from the warehouse.

Here the goods are transferred from the or election to the shipping or outbound area.

Selection activity basically involves selecting different materials and is grouped to meet the, customer demand. The idea of using warehouse as a selection area is to reduce the overall transportation cost.

4. **Shipping:** Shipping consists of checking and loading orders onto transportation vehicles. As in receiving, shipping is manually performed in most systems.

10 PRINCIPLES OF MATERIAL HANDLING

PLANNING PRINCIPLE

All material handling should be the result of a deliberate plan where the needs, performance objectives and functional specification of the proposed methods are completely defined at the outset.

Definition: *A plan is a prescribed course of action that is defined in advance of implementation. In its simplest form a material handing plan defines the material (what) and the moves (when and where); together they define the method (how and who).*

KEY POINTS:
The plan should be developed in consultation between the planner(s) and all who will use and benefit from the equipment to be employed.

Success in planning large scale material handling projects generally requires a team approach involving suppliers, consultants when appropriate, and end user specialists from management, engineering, computer and information systems, finance and operations.

The material handling plan should reflect the strategic objectives of the organization as well as the more immediate needs.

The plan should document existing methods and problems, physical and economic constraints, and future requirements and goals.

The plan should promote concurrent engineering of product, process design, process layout, and material handling methods, as opposed to independent and sequential design practices.

STANDARDIZATION PRINCIPLE

Material handling methods, equipment, controls and software should
be standardized within the limits of achieving overall performance objectives and without sacrificing needed flexibility , modularity and throughput anticipation of changing future requirements

Definition: *Standardization means less variety and customization in the methods and equipment employed.*

KEY POINTS:
The planner should select methods and equipment that can perform a variety of tasks under a variety of operating conditions and in Standardization applies to sizes of containers and other load forming components as well as operating procedures and equipment.
Standardization, flexibility and modularity must not be incompatible.

WORK PRINCIPLE

Material handling work should be minimized without sacrificing productivity or the level of service required of the operation.

Definition: *The measure of work is material handling flow (volume, weight or count per unit of time) multiplied by the distance moved.*

KEY POINTS:

Simplifying processes by reducing, combining, shortening or eliminating unnecessary moves will reduce work.

Consider each pickup and set-down, or placing material in and out of storage, as distinct moves and components of the distance moved.

Process methods, operation sequences and process/equipment layouts should be prepared that support the work minimization objective.

Where possible, gravity should be used to move materials or to assist in their movement while respecting consideration of safety and the potential for product damage.
The shortest distance between two points is a straight line

ERGONOMIC PRINCIPLE

Human capabilities and limitations must be recognized and respected in the design of material handling tasks and equipment to ensure safe and effective operations.

Definition: *Ergonomics is the science that seeks to adapt work or working conditions to suit the abilities of the worker.*

KEY POINTS:

Equipment should be selected that eliminates repetitive and strenuous manual labor and which effectively interacts with human operators and users.

The ergonomic principle embraces both physical and mental tasks.

The material handling workplace and the equipment employed to assist in that work must be designed so they are safe for people

UNIT LOAD PRINCIPLE

Unit loads shall be appropriately sized and configured in a way which achieves the material flow and inventory objectives at each stage in the supply chain.

Definition: *A unit load is one that can be stored or moved as a single entity at one time, such as a pallet, container or tote, regardless of the number of individual items that make up the load.*

KEY POINTS:

Less effort and work is required to collect and move many individual items as a single load than to move many items one at a time.
Load size and composition may change as material and product moves through stages of manufacturing and the resulting distribution
channels.
Large unit loads are common both pre and post manufacturing in the form of raw materials and finished goods.
During manufacturing, smaller unit loads, including as few as one item, yield less in-process inventory and shorter item throughput times.
Smaller unit loads are consistent with manufacturing strategies that embrace operating objectives such as flexibility, continuous flow and just-in-time delivery.
Unit loads composed of a mix of different items are consistent with just-in-time and/or customized supply strategies so long as item selectivity is not compromised.

SPACE UTILIZATION PRINCIPLE

Effective and efficient use must be made of all available space.

Definition: *Space in material handling is three dimensional and therefore is counted as cubic space.*

KEY POINTS:

In work areas, cluttered and unorganized spaces and blocked aisles should be eliminated.
In storage areas, the objective of maximizing storage density must be balanced against accessibility and selectivity.

When transporting loads within a facility the use of overhead space should be considered as an option.

SYSTEM PRINCIPLE

Material movement and storage activities should be fully integrated to form a coordinated, operational system which spans receiving, inspection, storage, production, assembly, packaging, unitizing, order selection, shipping, transportation and the handling of returns.

Definition: *A system is a collection of interacting and/or interdependent entities that form a unified whole.*

KEY POINTS:
Systems integration should encompass the entire supply chain including reverse logistics. It should include suppliers, manufacturers, distributors and customers.

Inventory levels should be minimized at all stages of production and distribution while respecting considerations of process variability
and customer service.

Information flow and physical material flow should be integrated and treated as concurrent activities Methods should be provided for easily
identifying materials and products, for determining their location and status within facilities and within the supply chain and for controlling their movement.

Customer requirements andregarding regarding quantity, quality, and on-time delivery should be met without exception. consitency and predictability, regarding quantity, quality, and on-time delivery should be met without exception.

KEY POINTS:
Pre-existing processes and methods should be simplified and/or re-engineered before any efforts at installing mechanized or automated systems.

Computerized material handling systems should be considered where appropriate for effective integration of material flow and information management.

Treat all interface issues as critical to successful automation, including equipment to equipment, equipment to load, equipment to operator, and control communications.

All items expected to be handled automatically must have features that accommodate mechanized and automated handling.

ENVIRONMENTAL PRINCIPLE

Environmental impact and energy consumption should be considered as criteria when designing or selecting alternative equipment and material handling systems.

Definition: *Environmental consciousness stems from a desire not to waste natural resources and to predict and eliminate the possible negative effects of our daily actions on the environment.*

KEY POINTS:

Containers, pallets and other products used to form and protect unit loads should be designed for reusability when possible and/or

biodegradability as appropriate. Systems design should accommodate

the handling of spent dunnage, empty containers and other by-products of material handling.

Materials specified as hazardous have special needs with regard to spill protection, combustibility and other risks.

AUTOMATION PRINCIPLE

Material handling operations should be mechanized and/or automated

where feasible to improve operational efficiency, increase responsiveness, improve consistency and predictability,

LIFE CYCLE COST NOTES PRINCIPLE

A thorough economic analysis should account for the entire life cycle of all material handling equipment and resulting systems.

Definition: *Life cycle costs include all cash flows new piece of equipment, or to put in place a new method, until that will occur between the time the first dollar is spent to plan or procure a that method and/or equipment is totally replaced.*

KEY POINTS:

Life cycle costs include capital investment, installation, setup and equipment programming, training, system testing and acceptance, operating (labor, utilities, etc.), maintenance and repair, reuse value, and ultimate disposal.

A plan for preventive and predictive maintenance should be prepared for the equipment, and the estimated cost of maintenance and spare parts should be included in the economic analysis.

A long-range plan for replacement of the equipment when it becomes obsolete should be prepared.

Although measurable cost is a primary factor, it is certainly not the only factor in selecting among alternatives. Other factors of a strategic nature to the organization and which form the basis for competition in the market place should be considered and quantified whenever possible.

<u>PRODUCTION PLANNING AND CONTROL</u>

In any manufacturing enterprise production is the driving force to which most other functions react.

This is particularly true with inventories; they exist because of the needs of production.

In this chapter the relationship of production planning and control to work-in-process inventories is stressed.

Objectives of Production Planning Control

- The ultimate objective of production planning and control, like that of all other manufacturing controls, is to contribute to the profits of the enterprise.

- As with inventory management and control, this is accomplished by keeping the customers satisfied through the meeting of delivery schedules.

- Specific objectives of production planning and control are to establish routes and schedules for work that will ensure the optimum utilization of materials, workers, and machines and to provide the means for ensuring the operation of the plant in accordance with these plans.

Production Planning and Control Functions

- All of the four basic phases of control of manufacture are easily identified in production planning and control.

- The plan for the processing of materials through the plant is established by the functions of process planning, loading, and scheduling. The function of dispatching puts the plan into effect; that is, operations are started in accordance with the plant.

- Actual performance is then compared to the planned performance, and, when required, corrective action is taken. In some instances re-planning is necessary to ensure the effective utilization of the manufacturing facilities and personnel.

Let us examine more closely each of these functions.

Process Planning (Routing)

The determination of where each operation on a component part, subassembly, or assembly is to be performed results in a route for the movement of a manufacturing lot through the factory.

Prior determination of these routes is the job of the manufacturing engineering function.

Loading

Once the route has been established, the work required can be loaded against the selected machine or workstation.

The total time required to perform the operation is computed by multiplying the unit operation times given on the standard process sheet by the number of parts to be processed.

This total time is then added to the work already planned for the workstation.

This is the function of loading, and it results in a tabulated list or chart showing the planned utilization of the machines or workstations in the plant.

Scheduling

Scheduling is the last of the planning functions. It determines when an operation is to be performed, or when work is to be completed; the difference lies in the detail of the scheduling procedure.

In a centralized control situation - where all process planning, loading, and scheduling for the plant are done in a central office- the details of the schedule may specify the starting and finishing time for an operation.

On the other hand, the central schedule may simply give a completion time for the work in a given department.

Combining Functions

While it is easy to define "where" as process planning, "how much work" as loading, and "when as scheduling, in actual operations these three functions are often combined and performed concurrently.

 How far in advance routes, loads, and schedules should be established always presents an interesting problem.

Obviously, it is desirable that a minimum of changes be made after schedules are established. This objective can be approached if the amount of work scheduled for the factory or department is equal to or slightly greater than the manufacturing cycle.

For optimum control, it should never be less than the manufacturing cycle.

Dispatching
Authorizing the start of an operation on the shop floor is the function of dispatching.
This function may be centralized or decentralized. Again using our machine-shop example, the departmental dispatcher would authorize the start of each of the three machine operations – three dispatch actions based on the foreman's routing and scheduling of the work through his department.
 This is decentralized dispatching.

Reporting or Follow – up
The manufacturing activity of a plant is said to be "in control" when the actual performance is within the objectives of the planned performance.
When jobs are started and completed on schedule, there should be very little, if any, concern about the meeting of commitments.

Optimum operation of the plant, however, is attained only if the original plan has been carefully prepared to utilize the manufacturing facilities fully and effectively.

Corrective Action

This is the keystone of any production planning and control activity. A plant in which all manufacturing activity runs on schedule in all probability is not being scheduled to its optimum productive capacity. With an optimum schedule, manufacturing delays are the rule, not the exception.

Re-planning

Re-planning is not corrective action. Re-planning revise routes, loads, and schedules; a new plan is developed. In manufacturing this is often required.

Changes in market conditions, manufacturing methods, or many other factors affecting the plant will often indicate that a new manufacturing plan is needed.

FACTORS AFFECTING PRODUCTION PLANNING AND CONTROL

The factors that affect the application of production planning and control to manufacturing are the same as the factors we have already discussed that affect inventory management and control.

Let us briefly review these in relation to production planning and control.

Type of Product

Again, it is the complexity of the product that is important, not what the product is, except as this may in turn relate to the market being served.
Production control procedures are much more complex and involve many more records in the manufacture of large steam turbine generator sets or locomotives to customer orders then in the production of large quantities of a standard product involving only a few component parts, such as electric blankets, steam irons, or similar small appliances.

Type of Manufacturing

This is probably the most influential factor in the control situation.
 For a large continuous manufacturing plant producing a standard product, we have already indicated that the routing was included in the planning of the plant layout.

PRODUCTION PLANNING AND CONTROL PROCEDURES

Though no production control function can be entirely eliminated, the least control that results in effective operation of the factory is the best control. It must be remembered that production planning and control systems should be tools of management. The objective is not an elaborate and detailed system of controls and records, but rather, the optimum operation of the plant for maximum profits.

Production Planning and Control Systems

Because production planning and control places an emphasis on the control of work-in-process, the system will in effect tie together all previous records and forms developed in all planning for the manufacture of the product.

Market forecast

The market forecast is discussed in Chapter 26. Its value to production planning and control is that it will indicate future trends in demand for manufactured product. Work shift policies, plans for an increase or decrease in manufacturing activity, or possible plant expansions may often be based upon the market forecasts and in turn affect the planning of the production planning and control group.

Sales Order

This is the second of the five classes of orders. It is a rewrite of the customer' order specifying what has been purchased – product and quantity and authorizing shipment of the goods to the customer.

Multiple copies are prepared and all interested functions are furnished a copy. Sales orders may be written by marketing, inventory control, or production control.

Stock Order

This third class of order is not always used. In the preceding paragraph we indicated how it may be used after sales order accumulate to an economical manufacturing lot.
It is, of course, the principal order when manufacturing to stock. It will authorize production in anticipation of future sales.

Shop Order

This fourth class of order deals with the manufacture of component parts. Customer orders, sales orders, and stock orders are for the finished product.

In the preceding chapters we discussed how, by product explosion, the requirements are established for component parts to build assembled products.

Standard Process sheet

This form is prepared by process engineering and it is the source of basic data as to the type of machine to be used, the time required for processing and the sequence of operations in the manufacture of the product. Routing and scheduling of shop orders, as well as loading of workstations in advance of scheduling, depend on up-to-date standard process sheets being available to the production planning and control group.

Engineering Specifications

Blueprints and bills of materials are used by production planning and control when they become a component part of the packaged instructions issued to the shop through the control office.

One good planning procedure is to accumulate all necessary data for a shop order in a single package the standard process sheet, the blueprint, the bill of material (if an assembly operation is involved), the route sheet, and possibly the schedule for the production of the order.

Route Sheet

This is the form on which the route of a shop order is indicated. In practice, this form is generally combined with one of the other forms in the system. For example, the shop order, the standard process sheet, and the route sheet are often one piece of paper- usually called the shop order or the manufacturing order.

Load Charts

These charts are prepared to show the productive capacity that has been "sold" – and at the same time the available productive capacity. These charts may be prepared for each workstation or machine in the plant, or they may be for groups of machines or departments.

Job Tickets

This is the fifth and last type of order in a manufacturing situation. Job tickets authorize the performance of individual operations in the manufacturing process.

Project Planning Methods

The production planning and control methods discussed thus far in this chapter deal primarily with the production of consumer or industrial products which could be considered to fall within the area of "repetitive manufacturing".

The products to be produced are often manufactured in quantities of more than one, and their total processing time can be measured in hours, or at most, days.

The best –known methods that have been developed are CPM (for Critical Path Method) and PERT (for Program Evaluation and Review Technique). The original

PERT technique is now considered, more accurately, PERT TIME, whereas a later development is known as PERT
COST.

From the optimistic, most likely, and pessimistic times, the expected elapsed time (te) can be obtained by statistical techniques. The relationship of the three estimates to the expected elapsed time is given by the formula

6a 4m b / te

Where a = optimistic time
b = pessimistic time
m = most likely time

It can be seen from the formula that the most likely time estimate is given four times as much weight as the optimistic and pessimistic estimates when computing the expected time.

Systems Analysis

As with other manufacturing control systems and procedures, production planning, and control lends itself to modern mechanization techniques such as machine accounting and use of computers.

Careful study of the control system through procedure analysis will indicate the savings that may be affected by the utilization of modern equipment.

These savings may be in the clerical help required in the administration of the system or in the advantages of quick compilation of data, which in turn results in up-to-date control data.

<u>SEQUENCING</u>

When more than one job is assigned to a machine or activity, the operator needs to know the order in which to process the jobs. The process of prioritizing jobs is called **sequencing.**

If no particular order is specified, the operator would probably process the job that arrived first. This default sequence is called *first-come, first-served* (FCFS). Or, if jobs are stacked upon arrival to a machine, it might be easier to process the job first that arrived last and is now on top of the stack. This is called *last-come, first-served* (LCFS) sequencing.

Another common approach is to process the job first that is due the soonest or the job that has the highest customer priority.

These are known as *earliest due date* (DDATE) and *highest customer priority* (CUSTPR) sequencing. Operators may also look through a stack of jobs to find one with a *similar setup* to the job that is currently being processed (SETUP).

That would minimize the downtime of the machine and make the operator's job easier.

Variations on the DDATE rule include *minimum slack* (SLACK) and *smallest critical ratio* (CR). SLACK considers the work remaining to be performed on a job as well as the time remaining (until the due date) to perform that work.

Jobs are processed first that have the least difference (or slack) between the two, as follows:

SLACK = (due date / today's date) / (remaining processing time)

The critical ratio uses the same information as SLACK but arranges it in ratio form so that scheduling performance can be easily assessed. Mathematically, the CR is calculated as follows:

$$CR = \frac{\text{time remaining}}{\text{work remaining}} = \frac{\text{due date} - \text{today's date}}{\text{remaining processing time}}$$

If the work remaining is greater than the time remaining, the critical ratio will be less than 1. If the time remaining is greater than the work remaining, the critical ratio will be greater than 1. If the time remaining equals work remaining, the critical ratio exactly equals 1.

The critical ratio allows us to make the following statements about our schedule:

If CR > 1, then the job is *ahead of schedule.*

If CR < 1, then the job is *behind schedule.*

If CR = 1, then the job is *exactly on schedule.*

Other sequencing rules examine processing time at a particular operation and order the work either by shortest processing time (SPT) or longest processing time (LPT).

LPT assumes long jobs are important jobs and is analogous to the strategy of doing larger tasks first to get them out of the way.

SPT focuses instead on shorter jobs and is able to complete many more jobs earlier than LPT.

With either rule, some jobs may be inordinately late because they are always put at the back of a queue.

All these "rules" for arranging jobs in a certain order for processing seem reasonable. We might wonder which methods are best or if it really matters which jobs are processed first anyway. Perhaps a few examples will help answer those questions.

SEQUENCING JOBS THROUGH ONE PROCESS

The simplest sequencing problem consists of a queue of jobs at one machine or process.

No new jobs arrive to the machine during the analysis, processing times and due dates are fixed, and setup time is considered negligible.

For this scenario, the *completion time* (also called **flow time**) of each job will differ depending on its place in the sequence, but the overall completion time for the set of jobs (called the **make span**), will not change.

Tardiness measures the difference between a job's due date and its completion time for those jobs completed after their due date.

Even in this simple case, there is no sequencing rule that optimizes both processing efficiency and due date performance.

SEQUENCING JOBS THROUGH TWO SERIAL PROCESSES

Since few factories consist of just one process, we might wonder if techniques exist that will produce an optimal sequence for any number of jobs processed through more than one machine or process.

Johnson's rule finds the fastest way to process a series of jobs through a two-machine system in which every job follows the same sequence through two machines.

Based on a variation of the SPT rule, it requires that the sequence be "mapped out" to determine the final completion time, or *make span,* for the set of jobs. The procedure is as follows:

1. List the time required to complete each job at each process. Set up a one-dimensional matrix to represent the desired sequence with the number of slots equal to the number of jobs.
2. Select the smallest processing time at either process. If that time occurs at process 1, put the associated job as near to the *beginning* of the sequence as possible.
3. If the smallest time occurs at process 2, put the associated job as near to the *end* of the sequence as possible.
4. Remove the job from the list.
5. Repeat steps 2-4 until all slots in the matrix have been filled or all jobs have been sequenced.

SEQUENCING JOBS THROUGH ANY NUMBER OF PROCESSES IN ANY ORDER

In a real-world job shop, jobs follow different routes through a facility that consists of many different machine centers or departments.

A small job shop may have three or four departments; a large job shop may have fifty or more.

From several to several hundred jobs may be circulating the shop at any given time. New jobs are released into the shop daily and placed in competition with existing jobs for priority in processing.

Queues form and dissipate as jobs move through the system. A dispatch list that shows the sequence in which jobs are to be processed at a particular machine may be valid at the beginning of a day or week but become outdated as new jobs arrive to the system.

Some jobs may have to wait to be assembled with others before continuing to be processed. Delays in completing operations can cause due dates to be revised and schedules changed.

In this enlarged setting, the types of sequencing rules used can be expanded. We can still use simple sequencing rules such as SPT, FCFS, and DDATE, but we can also conceive of more complex, or *global,* rules.

We may use FCFS to describe the arrival of jobs to a particular machine but *first-in-system, first-served* (FISFS) to differentiate the job's release into the system.

Giving a job top priority at one machine only to have it endure a lengthy wait at the next machine seems fruitless, so we might consider looking ahead to the next operation and sequencing the jobs in the current queue by smallest *work-in-next-queue* (WINQ).

We can create new rules such as *fewest number of operations remaining* (NOPN) or slack per remaining operation (S/OPN), which require updating as jobs progress through the system. *Remaining work* (RWK) is a variation of SPT that processes jobs by the smallest total processing time for *all* remaining operations, not just the current operation.

Any rule that has a remaining work component, such as SLACK or CR, needs to be updated as more operations of a job are completed. Thus, we need a mechanism for keeping track of and recording job progress.

Recall that MRP systems can be used to change due dates, release orders, and, in general, coordinate production.

Many of the rules described in this section are options in the shop floor module of standard MRP packages.
Critical ratio is especially popular for use in conjunction with MRP.

The complexity and dynamic nature of the scheduling environment precludes the use of analytical solution techniques.

The most popular form of analysis for these systems is simulation. Academia has especially enjoyed creating and testing sequencing rules in simulations of hypothetical job shops.

One early simulation study alone examined ninety-two different sequencing rules. Although no optimum solutions have been identified in these simulation studies, they have produced some general guidelines for *when* certain sequencing rules may be appropriate.

Here are a few of their suggestions:

1. *SPT is most useful when the shop is highly congested.* SPT tends to minimize mean flow time, mean number of jobs in the system (and thus work-in-process inventory), and percent of jobs tardy.

   By completing more jobs quickly, it theoretically satisfies a greater number of customers than the other rules.

   However, with SPT some long jobs may be completed *very* late, resulting in a small number of very unsatisfied customers.

   For this reason, when SPT is used in practice, it is usually truncated (or stopped), depending on the amount of time a job has been waiting or the nearness of its due date.

For example, many mainframe computer systems process jobs by SPT. Jobs that are submitted are placed in several categories (A, B, or C) based on expected CPU time.

The shorter jobs, or A jobs, are processed first, but every couple of hours the system stops processing A jobs and picks the first job from the B stack to run.

After the B job is finished, the system returns to the A stack and continues processing. C jobs may be processed only once a day.

Other systems that have access to due date information will keep a long job waiting until its SLACK is zero or its due date is within a certain range.

2. *Use SLACK or S/OPN for periods of normal activity.* When capacity is not severely restrained, a SLACK-oriented rule that takes into account both due date and processing time will produce good results.
3. *Use DDATE when only small tardiness values can be tolerated.* DDATE tends to minimize mean tardiness and maximum tardiness. Although more jobs will be tardy under DDATE than SPT, the degree of tardiness will be much less.
4. *Use LPT if subcontracting is anticipated* so that larger jobs are completed in-house, and smaller jobs are sent out as their due date draws near.
5. *Use FCFS when operating at low-capacity levels.* FCFS allows the shop to operate essentially without sequencing jobs. When the workload at a facility is light, any sequencing rule will do, and FCFS is certainly the easiest to apply.

Do not use SPT to sequence jobs that have to be assembled with other jobs at a later date. For assembly jobs, a sequencing rule that gives a common priority to the processing of different components in an assembly, such as *assembly DDATE,* produces a more effective schedule.

<u>PERT/CPM FOR PROJECT SCHEDULING & MANAGEMENT</u>

1. INTRODUCTION

Basically, CPM (Critical Path Method) and PERT (Programme Evaluation Review Technique) are project management techniques, which have been created out of the need of Western industrial and military establishments to plan, schedule and control complex projects.

1.1 Brief History of CPM/PERT

- CPM/PERT or Network Analysis as the technique is sometimes called, developed along two parallel streams, one industrial and the other military.
- CPM was the discovery of M.R.Walker of E.I.Du Pont de Nemours & Co. and J.E.Kelly of Remington Rand, circa 1957.
- The computation was designed for the UNIVAC-I computer. The first test was made in 1958, when CPM was applied to the construction of a new chemical plant.
- In March 1959, the method was applied to a maintenance shut-down at the Du Pont works in Louisville, Kentucky. Unproductive time was reduced from 125 to 93 hours.
- PERT was devised in 1958 for the POLARIS missile program by the Program Evaluation Branch of the Special Projects office of the U.S.Navy, helped by the Lockheed Missile Systems division and the Consultant firm of Booz-Allen & Hamilton.
- The calculations were so arranged so that they could be carried out on the IBM Naval Ordinance Research Computer (NORC) at Dahlgren, Virginia.

1.2 Planning, Scheduling & Control

- Planning, Scheduling (or organising) and Control are considered to be basic Managerial functions, and CPM/PERT has been rightfully accorded due importance in the literature on Operations Research and Quantitative Analysis.

- Far more than the technical benefits, it was found that PERT/CPM provided a focus around which managers could brain-storm and put their ideas together.
- It proved to be a great communication medium by which thinkers and planners at one level could communicate their ideas, their doubts and fears to another level.
- Most important, it became a useful tool for evaluating the performance of individuals and teams.
- There are many variations of CPM/PERT which have been useful in planning costs, scheduling manpower and machine time.

CPM/PERT can answer the following important questions:

How long will the entire project take to be completed? What are the risks involved?

Which are the critical activities or tasks in the project which could delay the entire project if they were not completed on time?

Is the project on schedule, behind schedule or ahead of schedule?

If the project has to be finished earlier than planned, what is the best way to do this at the least cost?

1.3 The Framework for PERT and CPM

Essentially, there are six steps which are common to both the techniques. The procedure is listed below:

I. Define the Project and all of it's significant activities or tasks. The Project (made up of several tasks) should have only a single start activity and a single finish activity.

II. Develop the relationships among the activities. Decide which activities must precede and which must follow others.

III. Draw the "Network" connecting all the activities. Each Activity should have unique event numbers. Dummy arrows are used where required to avoid giving the same numbering to two activities.

IV.   Assign time and/or cost estimates to each activity

V.   Compute the longest time path through the network. This is called the critical path.

VI.   Use the Network to help plan, schedule, monitor and control the project.

The Key Concept used by CPM/PERT is that a small set of activities, which make up the longest path through the activity network control the entire project.

If these "critical" activities could be identified and assigned to responsible persons, management resources could be optimally used by concentrating on the few activities which determine the fate of the entire project.

Non-critical activities can be replanned, rescheduled and resources for them can be reallocated flexibly, without affecting the whole project.

Five useful questions to ask when preparing an activity network are:

- Is this a Start Activity?
- Is this a Finish Activity?
- What Activity Precedes this?
- What Activity Follows this?
- What Activity is Concurrent with this?

Some activities are serially linked. The second activity can begin only after the first activity is completed.

In certain cases, the activities are concurrent, because they are independent of each other and can start simultaneously.

This is especially the case in organisations which have supervisory resources so that work can be delegated to various departments which will be responsible for the activities and their completion as planned.

When work is delegated like this, the need for constant feedback and co-ordination becomes an important senior management pre-occupation.

1.4 Drawing the CPM/PERT Network

Each activity (or sub-project) in a PERT/CPM Network is represented by an arrow symbol. Each activity is preceded and succeeded by an event, represented as a circle and numbered.

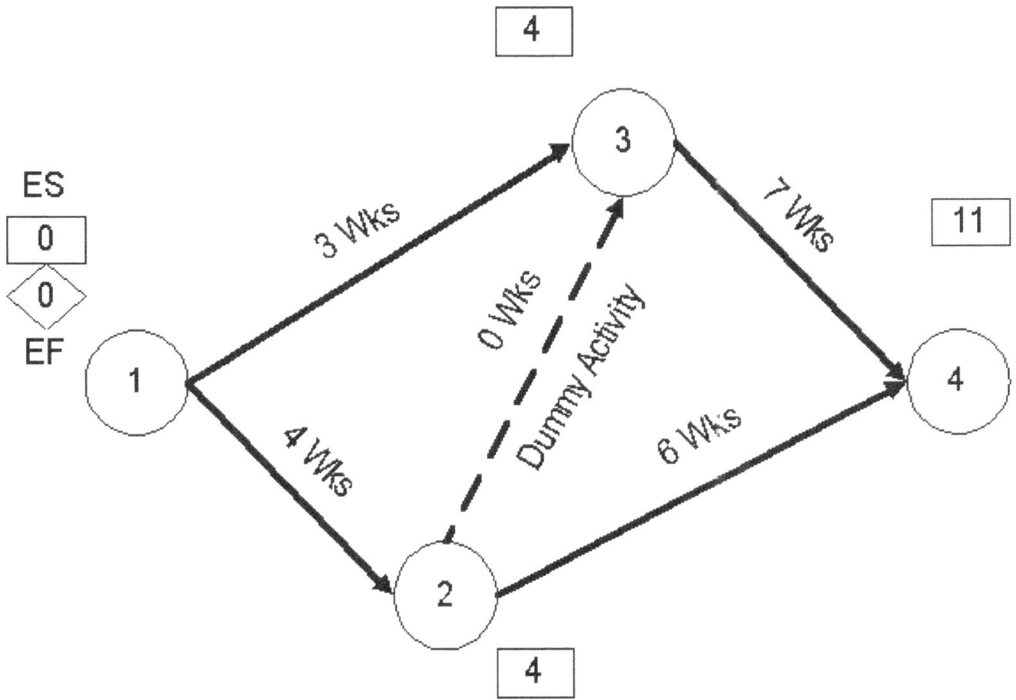

At Event 3, we have to evaluate two predecessor activities - Activity 1-3 and Activity 2-3, both of which are predecessor activities. Activity 1-3 gives us an Earliest Start of 3 weeks at Event 3. However, Activity 2-3 also has to be completed before Event 3 can begin. Along this route, the Earliest Start would be 4+0=4. The rule is to take the longer (bigger) of the two Earliest Starts. So the Earliest Start at event 3 is 4.

Similarly, at Event 4, we find we have to evaluate two predecessor activities - Activity 2-4 and Activity 3-4. Along Activity 2-4, the Earliest Start at Event 4 would be 10 wks, but along Activity 3-4, the Earliest Start at Event 4 would be 11 wks. Since 11 wks is larger than 10 wks, we select it as the Earliest Start at Event 4.**We have now found the longest path through the network. It will take 11 weeks along activities 1-2, 2-3 and 3-4. This is the Critical Path.**

1.5.3 The Backward Pass - Latest Finish Time Rule

To make the Backward Pass, we begin at the sink or the final event and work backwards to the first event.

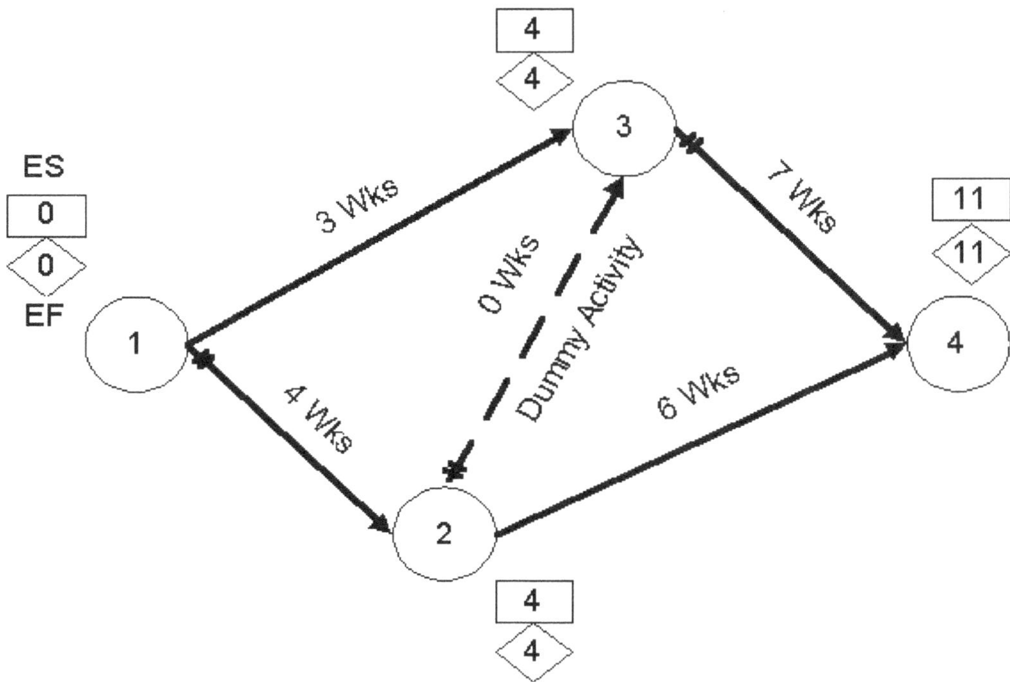

At Event 3 there is only one activity, Activity 3-4 in the backward pass, and we find that the value is 11-7 = 4 weeks. However at Event 2 we have to evaluate 2 activities, 2-3 and 2-4. We find that the backward pass through 2-4 gives us a value of 11-6 = 5 while 2-3 gives us 4-0 = 4. We take the **smaller value** of 4 on the backward pass.

1.5.4 Tabulation & Analysis of Activities

We are now ready to tabulate the various events and calculate the Earliest and Latest Start and Finish times. We are also now ready to compute the SLACK or TOTAL FLOAT, which is defined as the difference between the Latest Start and Earliest Start.

Event	Duration(Weeks)	Earliest Start	Earliest Finish	Latest Start	Latest Finish	Total Float
1-2	4	0	4	0	4	0
2-3	0	4	4	4	4	0
3-4	7	4	11	4	11	0
1-3	3	0	3	1	4	1
2-4	6	4	10	5	11	1

- The Earliest Start is the value in the rectangle near the tail of each activity
- The Earliest Finish is = Earliest Start + Duration
- The Latest Finish is the value in the diamond at the head of each activity
- The Latest Start is = Latest Finish - Duration

There are two important types of Float or Slack. These are Total Float and Free Float.

TOTAL FLOAT is the spare time available when all preceding activities occur at the **earliest** possible times and all succeeding activities occur at the **latest** possible times.

- Total Float = Latest Start - Earliest Start

Activities with zero Total float are on the Critical Path

FREE FLOAT is the spare time available when all preceding activities occur at the **earliest** possible times and all succeeding activities occur at the **earliest** possible times.

When an activity has zero Total float, Free float will also be zero.

There are various other types of float (Independent, Early Free, Early Interfering, Late Free, Late Interfering), and float can also be negative. We shall not go into these situations at present for the sake of simplicity and be concerned only with Total Float for the time being.

Having computed the various parameters of each activity, we are now ready to go into the scheduling phase, using a type of bar chart known as the Gantt Chart.

There are various other types of float (Independent, Early Free, Early Interfering, Late Free, Late Interfering), and float can also be negative. We shall not go into these situations at present for the sake of simplicity and be concerned only with Total Float for the time being. Having computed the various parameters of each activity, we are now ready to go into the scheduling phase, using a type of bar chart known as the Gantt Chart.

1.5.5 Scheduling of Activities Using a Gantt Chart

Once the activities are laid out along a Gantt Chart (Please see chart below), the concepts of Earliest Start & Finish, Latest Start & Finish and Float will become very obvious.

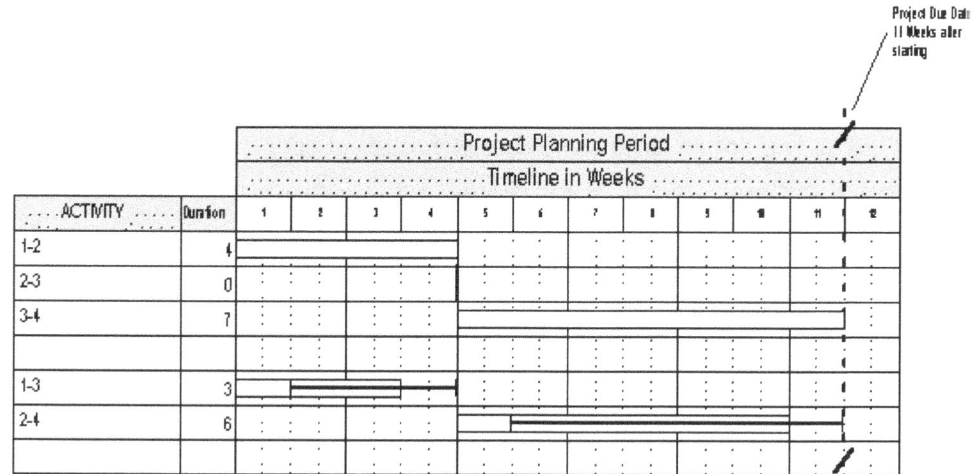

Activities 1-3 and 2-4 have total float of 1 week each, represented by the solid timeline which begins at the latest start and ends at the latest finish. The difference is the float, which gives us the flexibility to schedule the activity.

For example, we might send the staff on leave during that one week or give them some other work to do. Or we may choose to start the activity slightly later than planned, knowing that we have a week's float in hand. We might even break the activity in the middle (if this is permitted) for a week and divert the staff for some other work, or declare a National or Festival holiday as required under the National and Festival Holidays Act.

These are some of the examples of the use of float to schedule an activity. Once all the activities that can be scheduled are scheduled to the convenience of the project, normally reflecting resource optimisation measures, we can say that the project has been scheduled.

2. Exercise

A Social Project manager is faced with a project with the following activities:

Activity-id	Activity - Description	Duration
1-2	Social Work Team to live in Village	5 Weeks
1-3	Social Research Team to do survey	12 Weeks
3-4	Analyse results of survey	5 Weeks
2-4	Establish Mother & Child Health Program	14 Weeks
3-5	Establish Rural Credit	15 Weeks

Programme

4-5   Carry out Immunisation of   4 Weeks
Under Fives

- Draw the arrow diagram, using the helpful numbering of the activities, which suggests the following logic:
- Unless the Social Work team lives in the village, the Mother and Child Health Programme cannot be started due to ignorance and superstition of the villagers
- The Analysis of the survey can obviously be done only after the survey is complete.
- Until rural survey is done, the Rural Credit Programme cannot be started
- Unless Mother and Child Programme is established, the Immunisation of Under Fives cannot be started
- - Calculate the Earliest and Latest Event Times
- - Tabulate and Analyse the Activities
- - Schedule the Project Using a Gantt Chart

3. The PERT (Probabilistic) Approach

So far we have talked about projects, where there is high certainty about the outcomes of activities. In other words, the cause-effect logic is well known. This is particularly the case in Engineering projects.

However, in Research & Development projects, or in Social Projects which are defined as "Process Projects", where learning is an important outcome, the cause-effect relationship is not so well established.

In such situations, the PERT approach is useful, because it can accommodate the variation in event completion times, based on an expert's or an expert committee's estimates.

For each activity, three time estimates are taken

- The Most Optimistic
- The Most Likely

- The Most Pessimistic

The Duration of an activity is calculated using the following formula:

$$t_e = \frac{t_o + 4t_m + t_p}{6}$$

Where t_e is the Expected time, t_o is the Optimistic time, t_m is the most probable activity time and t_p is the Pessimistic time.

It is not necessary to go into the theory behind the formula. It is enough to know that the weights are based on an approximation of the Beta distribution.

The Standard Deviation, which is a good measure of the variability of each activity is calculated by the rather simplified formula:

$$s_t = \frac{t_p - t_o}{6}$$

The Variance is the Square of the Standard Deviation.

4. PERT Calculations for the Social Project

In our Social Project, the Project Manager is now not so certain that each activity will be completed on the basis of the single estimate he gave. There are many assumptions involved in each estimate, and these assumptions are illustrated in the three-time estimate he would prefer to give to each activity.

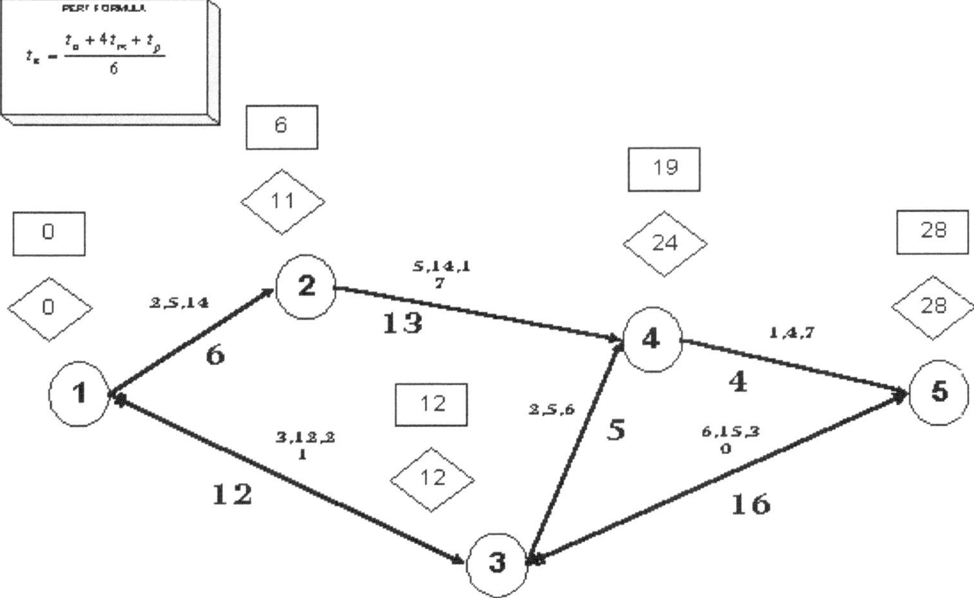

In Activity 1-3, the time estimates are 3,12 and 21. Using our PERT formula, we get:

$$t_e = \frac{3 + (4 \times 12) + 21}{6} = \frac{72}{6} = 12$$

$$s_1 = \frac{(21-3)}{6} = \frac{18}{6} = 3$$

The Standard Deviation (s.d.) for this activity is also calculated using the PERT formula

We calculate the PERT event times and other details as below for each activity:

Event	t_o	t_m	t_p	t_e	ES	EF	LS	LF	TF	s.d.	Var.
1-3	3	12	21	12	0	12	0	12	0	3	9

3-5	6	15	30	16	12	28	12	28	0	4	16
1-2	2	5	14	6	0	6	5	11	5	2	4
2-4	5	14	17	13	6	19	11	24	5	2	4
3-4	2	5	8	5	12	17	19	24	7	1	1
4-5	1	4	7	4	19	23	24	28	5	1	1

5. Estimating Risk

Having calculated the s.d. and the Variance, we are ready to do some risk analysis. Before that we should be aware of two of the most important assumptions made by PERT.

- The Beta distribution is appropriate for calculation of activity durations.

- Activities are independent, and the time required to complete one activity has no bearing on the completion times of it's successor activities in the network. The validity of this assumption is questionable when we consider that in practice, many activities have dependencies.

The project manager is confronted with having to reduce the scheduled completion time of a project to meet a deadline.

Project duration can often be reduced by assigning more labor to project activities, in the form of over time, and by assigning more resources, such as material, equipment, etc.

However, the additional labor and resources increase the project cost.

So, the decision to reduce the project duration must based on an analysis of the trade-off between time and cost.

PROJECT CRASHING

The goal of crashing is to reduce project duration at minimum cost.

To reduce project duration while minimizing the cost of crashing, the project team should estimate require time, require the cost, crash time, crash cost for each activities.

And then the team can estimate total crash time, total crash cost, the crash cost per week to reduce project duration at minimum cost.

Project crashing is a method for shortening the project duration by reducing the time of one or more of the critical project activities to less than its normal activity time. The object crashing is to reduce project duration while minimizing the cost of crashing.

OBJECTIVE OF CRASHING

1. To reduce the scheduled completion time to reap the results of the project sooner.
2. As project continue over time, the team consume indirect costs.
3. There may be direct financial penalties for not completing a project on time.

<u>WHAT IS ISO?</u>

ISO is an International Organization for Standards that was formed by technical committees.

They provide user-friendly guidelines for a wide range of organizations. Examples of these organizations include manufacturing, processing, servicing, printing, forestry, and electronics.

ISO was established in 1947, in Switzerland, with the purpose of developing intellectual, scientific, technological, and economic corporation between member countries (Bureau of Business Practice).

Later in 1979 the ISO Technical Committee (ISO/TC 176) was formed to make a set of guidelines that would bring together and standardize world industries.

ISO has affiliates in more than 90 countries. It is interesting to note that ISO comes from the Greek word "isos" which means "same as." The words "same as" can be implied to mean the consumer gets what the consumer expects.

In our quality assurance class we have learned that if the consumer gets what they expect, this is consider quality. Therefore, the root word ISO stands for quality.

WHAT IS ISO 9000?

ISO 9000 is a set of five International Standards for Quality Assurance.
- ISO 9000 contains guidelines for the other four standards.
- ISO 9001 is intended for suppliers who do a lot of design or customization.
- ISO 9002 involves standards for both production and installation.
- ISO 9003 is guidelines for final test and inspection.
- ISO 9004 is designed to help managers develop a substantial quality system (Bureau of Business Practice).

The ISO 9000 standards are not rules, but merely a set of guidelines that organize their processes and make it more cost effective

HOW DOES THE SERIES ON 9000 WORK?

As businesses change and become more complex, ISO has adapted to meet these demands.

ISO has come up with 9001, 9002, 9003 etc. to cover different aspects of the business.

Even the United States government has adopted ISO standards with the ANSI/ASQC Q9000 series.

WHAT IS THE DIFFERENCE BETWEEN ISO 9000 AND OTHER QUALITY CONTROL AWARDS.

The purpose behind these awards is to bring total quality to a product. By following the ISO 9000 guidelines, companies will have an excellent start on quality assurance models.

For example, companies that have previously received the Malcolm Baldrige National Quality Award have applied those criteria to their operations.

However, those companies who have applied the ISO 9000 guidelines into their operations have reaped additional benefits. By applying both criteria to their operations, companies are able to achieve total quality (Bureau of Business Practice).

The foundation that ISO 9000 provides will better prepare companies for those Quality Control Awards.

SO, WHAT DOES IT MEAN TO BE ISO CERTIFIED?

Often companies become ISO certified because customers require it.

For example, a lot of customers in Europe demand ISO 9000 approval. Where some companies miss out is when they only get ISO 9000 certified for marketing reasons.

The ISO 9000 standards improve operating procedure and reduce cost. Being ISO certified means that companies operate using the ISO guideline. When companies advertise the fact that they are ISO certified, it has been proven to be a very powerful marketing tool for them. When customers know that their product is ISO 9000 certified they feel assured that their product is what they expect.

These stamp of ISO 9000 approval, lets customers know what to expect, thus they get a quality product. The standards set by ISO 9000 insure a dependable Quality Assurance system. Additionally, any company that does business in Europe knows that customers are demanding products be ISO 9000 certified.

As worldwide customers demand ISO 9000 standards, ISO 9000 will become more prevalent. As more international companies come into the market, this will make companies more competitive.

The increase in competition will improve the quality and decrease cost of the product, thus creating a better environment for the consumer.

WHAT ARE SOME EXAMPLES OF ISO 9000 USES IN INDUSTRY?

Measurement and calibration is one of the most important elements in quality assurance. ISO 9001-9003 lay down some procedures to be followed when selecting, using, calibrating, controlling, and maintaining measurement standards for measuring equipment.

For instance, ISO specifies that each instrument must have a label to show calibration status, usage limits, and any instrument that has failed or suspected to be out of calibration.

If an instrument fails this specification, it must be withdrawn from use and labeled conspicuously to prevent accidental use (Morris 10). The procedures in ISO 9001-90003 can be used to ensure the quality of their products.

It also states that all calibration procedures must be documented, all personnel performing calibration function must have adequate training, and adjustable devices must be sealed to prevent tampering (Morris 9).

These stated procedures are intended to prevent errors that are caused by operators. The procedures also improve the confidence level of the data.

By improving the confidence level of the data, companies will be able to see when a problem appears in production within a short period of time. Fast response time to problems will equal more profit for the company.

WHAT ARE THE DISADVANTAGES OF ISO 9000?

Many companies are ISO 9000, but there are some companies that choose not to be certified. As previously stated, ISO 9000 is a stead of guidelines.

These guidelines are implemented into companies operations. However, there are reasons why companies would not be ISO.

The actual change of operations can be very expensive. Usually designated people have to take classes and be trained as the company's liaison for ISO 9000.

These people, as part of their full time jobs, train fellow employees how to implement and use ISO 9000 procedures.

As is well known in business and industry, it is difficult to change the habits of longtime employees. New procedures are rarely welcomed with open arms. In fact, new ways are usually resisted by everyone. This resistance cuts into profits and also decreases company morale.

There are times when companies feel that the existing set of operational procedures is already working well and they do not feel a change is necessary.

Frequently, companies will have a customer who demands that they be ISO 9000 certified to continue doing business.

Now the company has the choice of loosing a customer or implementing ISO 9000. Either way money is lost in the short term.

Even though there may be an initial implementing cost, ISO 9000 has been proven to reduce cost and improve the total quality in the long rur.

The implementation of ISO 9000 benefits far out weight any disadvantages.

WHAT ARE THE ADVANTAGES TO HAVING A QUALITY SYSTEM?

Companies strive for a total quality systems because quality is what the customer demands.
There are other reasons why a company may seek a quality system.
- Ensure that products and services provided meet customer requirements.
- Ensure consistency in the day to day operations.
- Ensure that processes are repeatable and predictable.
- Allow the company to create and retain satisfied customers
- Improve the efficiency, reduce operating cost and minimize unproductive time.

All of these features are important in having a competitive company.
ISO 9000 is not just a badge to be worn, it is a set of standards to be followed.

It is quickly sweeping the world as an international standard. Those companies who ignore ISO 9000 will be left behind. The advantages far out weight the disadvantages, if a company follows the ISO 9000 guidelines strictly.

So what does it mean to be ISO 9000 certified? It means following the ISO 9000 guidelines to build a competitive company in a global economy.

<u>JUST IN TIME (BUSINESS)</u>

- **Just in time** (**JIT**) is a production strategy that strives to improve a business' return on investment by reducing in-process inventory and associated carrying costs.

- To meet JIT objectives, the process relies on signals or Kanban (看板?, Kanban) between different points, which are involved in the process, which tell production when to make the next part.

- Kanban are usually 'tickets' but can be simple visual signals, such as the presence or absence of a part on a shelf. Implemented correctly, JIT focuses on continuous improvement and can improve a manufacturing organization's return on investment, quality, and efficiency.

- To achieve continuous improvement key areas of focus could be flow, employee involvement and quality.

- JIT relies on other elements in the inventory chain as well. For instance, its effective application cannot be independent of other key components of a lean manufacturing system or it can "end up with the opposite of the desired result."

- In recent years manufacturers have continued to try to hone forecasting methods such as applying a trailing 13-week average as a better predictor for JIT planning; however, some research demonstrates that basing JIT on the presumption of stability is inherently flawed.

Effects

- A surprising effect of JIT was that car factory response time fell to about a day. This improved customer satisfaction by providing vehicles within a day or two of the minimum economic shipping delay.

- Also, the factory began building many vehicles to order, eliminating the risk they would not be sold. This improved the company's return on equity.

- Since assemblers no longer had a choice of which part to use, every part had to fit perfectly. This caused a quality assurance crisis, which led to a dramatic improvement in product quality.

- Eventually, Toyota redesigned every part of its vehicles to widen tolerances, while simultaneously implementing careful statistical controls for quality control.

- Toyota had to test and train parts suppliers to assure quality and delivery. In some cases, the company eliminated multiple suppliers.
- When a process or parts quality problem surfaced on the production line, the entire production line had to be slowed or even stopped. No inventory meant a line could not operate from in-process inventory while a production problem was fixed.
- Many people in Toyota predicted that the initiative would be abandoned for this reason. In the first week, line stops occurred almost hourly. But by the end of the first month, the rate had fallen to a few line stops per day.
- After six months, line stops had so little economic effect that Toyota installed an overhead pull-line, similar to a bus bell-pull, that let any worker on the line order a line stop for a process or quality problem. Even with this, line stops fell to a few per week.
- The result was a factory that has been studied worldwide. It has been widely emulated, but not always with the expected results, as many firms fail to adopt the full system.
- The just-in-time philosophy was also applied to other segments of the supply chain in several types of industries. In the commercial sector, it meant eliminating one or all of the warehouses in the link between a factory and a retail establishment.
- Examples in sales, marketing, and customer service involve applying information systems and mobile hardware to deliver customer information as needed, and reducing waste by video conferencing to cut travel time.

Benefits

Main benefits of JIT include:

- *Reduced setup time.* Cutting setup time allows the company to reduce or eliminate inventory for "changeover" time. The tool used here is SMED (single-minute exchange of dies).
- *The flow of goods from warehouse to shelves improves.* Small or individual piece lot sizes reduce lot delay inventories, which simplifies inventory flow and its management.
- *Employees with multiple skills are used more efficiently.* Having employees trained to work on different parts of the process allows companies to move workers where they are needed.

- *Production scheduling and work hour consistency synchronized with demand.* If there is no demand for a product at the time, it is not made. This saves the company money, either by not having to pay workers overtime or by having them focus on other work or participate in training.
- *Increased emphasis on supplier relationships.* A company without inventory does not want a supply system problem that creates a part shortage. This makes supplier relationships extremely important.
- *Supplies come in at regular intervals throughout the production day.* Supply is synchronized with production demand and the optimal amount of inventory is on hand at any time. When parts move directly from the truck to the point of assembly, the need for storage facilities is reduced.
- *Minimizes storage space needed.*
- *Smaller chance of inventory breaking/expiring.*

Problems

Within a JIT system

- Just-in-time operation leaves suppliers and downstream consumers open to supply shocks and large supply or demand changes. For internal reasons, Ohno saw this as a feature rather than a bug.
- He used an analogy of lowering the water level in a river to expose the rocks to explain how removing inventory showed where production flow was interrupted.
- Once barriers were exposed, they could be removed. Since one of the main barriers was rework, lowering inventory forced each shop to improve its own quality or cause a holdup downstream.
- A key tool to manage this weakness is production levelling to remove these variations. Just-in-time is a means to improving performance of the system, not an end.
- Very low stock levels means shipments of the same part can come in several times per day. This means Toyota is especially susceptible to flow interruption. For that reason, Toyota uses two suppliers for most assemblies.
- As noted in Liker (2003), there was an exception to this rule that put the entire company at risk because of the 1997 Aisin fire. However, since Toyota also makes a point of maintaining high quality relations with its entire supplier network, several other suppliers immediately took up production of the Aisin-built parts by using existing capability and documentation.

LEAN MANUFACTURING

- **Lean manufacturing**, **lean enterprise**, or **lean production**, often simply, "**lean**", is a production practice that considers the expenditure of resources for any goal other than the creation of value for the end customer to be wasteful, and thus a target for elimination.
- Working from the perspective of the customer who consumes a product or service, "value" is defined as any action or process that a customer would be willing to pay for.
- Essentially, lean is centered on *preserving value with less work*. Lean manufacturing is a management philosophy derived mostly from the Toyota Production System (TPS) (hence the term Toyotism is also prevalent) and identified as "lean" only in the 1990s.
- TPS is renowned for its focus on reduction of the original Toyota *seven wastes* to improve overall customer value, but there are varying perspectives on how this is best achieved.
- The steady growth of Toyota, from a small company to the world's largest automaker, has focused attention on how it has achieved this success.

Overview

- Lean principles are derived from the Japanese manufacturing industry. The term was first coined by John Krafcik in his 1988 article, "Triumph of the Lean Production System," based on his master's thesis at the MIT Sloan School of Management.
- Krafcik had been a quality engineer in the Toyota-GM NUMMI joint venture in California before coming to MIT for MBA studies. Krafcik's research was continued by the International Motor Vehicle Program (IMVP) at MIT, which produced the international best-seller book co-authored by Jim Womack, Daniel Jones, and Daniel Roos called *The Machine That Changed the World.*
- A complete historical account of the IMVP and how the term "lean" was coined is given by Holweg (2007).
- For many, lean is the set of "tools" that assist in the identification and steady elimination of waste (*muda*). As waste is eliminated quality improves while production time and cost are reduced.
- A non exhaustive list of such tools would include: SMED, Value Stream Mapping, Five S, *Kanban* (pull systems), *poka-yoke* (error-proofing), Total Productive Maintenance, elimination of time batching, mixed model processing, Rank Order

Clustering, single point scheduling, redesigning working cells, multi-process handling and control charts (for checking mura).

- There is a second approach to lean Manufacturing, which is promoted by Toyota, called The Toyota Way, in which the focus is upon improving the "flow" or smoothness of work, thereby steadily eliminating *mura* ("unevenness") through the system and not upon 'waste reduction' per se.
- Techniques to improve flow include production leveling, "pull" production (by means of *kanban*) and the *Heijunka box.*
- This is a fundamentally different approach from most improvement methodologies, which may partially account for its lack of popularity.
- The difference between these two approaches is not the goal itself, but rather the prime approach to achieving it.
- The implementation of smooth flow exposes quality problems that already existed, and thus waste reduction naturally happens as a consequence. The advantage claimed for this approach is that it naturally takes a system-wide perspective, whereas a waste focus sometimes wrongly assumes this perspective.
- Both lean and TPS can be seen as a loosely connected set of potentially competing principles whose goal is cost reduction by the elimination of waste. These principles include: Pull processing, Perfect first-time quality, Waste minimization, Continuous improvement, Flexibility, Building and maintaining a long term relationship with suppliers, Autonomation, Load leveling and Production flow and Visual control.
- The disconnected nature of some of these principles perhaps springs from the fact that the TPS has grown pragmatically since 1948 as it responded to the problems it saw within its own production facilities.
- Thus what one sees today is the result of a 'need' driven learning to improve where each step has built on previous ideas and not something based upon a theoretical framework.
- Toyota's view is that the main method of lean is not the tools, but the reduction of three types of waste: *muda* ("non-value-adding work"), *muri* ("overburden"), and *mura* ("unevenness"), to expose problems systematically and to use the tools where the ideal cannot be achieved.
- From this perspective, the tools are workarounds adapted to different situations, which explains any apparent incoherence of the principles above.

QUALITY MANAGEMENT

- The term *quality management* has a specific meaning within many business sectors.

- This specific definition, which does not aim to assure 'good quality' by the more general definition, but rather to ensure that an organization or product is consistent, can be considered to have four main components: quality planning, quality control, quality assurance and quality improvement.

- Quality management is focused not only on product/service quality, but also the means to achieve it.

- Quality management therefore uses quality assurance and control of processes as well as products to achieve more consistent quality.

PRINCIPLES

The International Standard for Quality management (ISO 9001:2008) adopts a number of management principles that can be used by top management to guide their organizations towards improved performance. The principles include:

Customer focus

since the organizations depend on their customers, they should understand current and future customer needs, should meet customer requirements and should try to exceed the expectations of customers. An organization attains customer focus when all people in the organization know both the internal and external customers and also what customer requirements must be met to ensure that both the internal and external customers are satisfied.

Leadership

Leaders of an organization establish unity of purpose and direction of it. They should go for creation and maintenance of such an internal environment, in which people can become fully involved in achieving the organization's quality objective.

Involvement of people

People at all levels of an organization are the essence of it. Their complete involvement enables their abilities to be used for the benefit of the organization.

Process approach

The desired result can be achieved when activities and related resources are managed in an organization as process. This may also affect it

System approach to management

An organization's effectiveness and efficiency in achieving its quality objectives are contributed by identifying, understanding and managing all interrelated processes as a system. Quality Control involves checking transformed and transforming resources in all stages of production process.

Continual improvement

One of the permanent quality objectives of an organization should be the continual improvement of its overall performance.

Factual approach to decision making

Effective decisions are always based on the data analysis and information.

Mutually beneficial supplier relationships

Since an organization and its suppliers are interdependent, therefore a mutually beneficial relationship between them increases the ability of both to add value.

These eight principles form the basis for the quality management system standard ISO 9001:2008.

Quality improvement

There are many methods for quality improvement. These cover product improvement, process improvement and people based improvement. In the following list are methods of quality management and techniques that incorporate and drive quality improvement:

1. ISO 9004:2008 — guidelines for performance improvement.
2. ISO 15504-4: 2005 — information technology — process assessment — Part 4: Guidance on use for process improvement and process capability determination.
3. QFD — quality function deployment, also known as the house of quality approach.
4. Kaizen — 改善, Japanese for change for the better; the common English term is *continuous improvement*.
5. Zero Defect Program — created by NEC Corporation of Japan, based upon statistical process control and one of the inputs for the inventors of Six Sigma.
6. Six Sigma — 6σ, Six Sigma combines established methods such as statistical process control, design of experiments and failure mode and effects analysis (FMEA) in an overall framework.
7. PDCA — plan, do, check, act cycle for quality control purposes. (Six Sigma's DMAIC method (define, measure, analyze, improve, control) may be viewed as a particular implementation of this.)
8. Quality circle — a group (people oriented) approach to improvement.
9. Taguchi methods — statistical oriented methods including quality robustness, quality loss function, and target specifications.
10. The Toyota Production System — reworked in the west into lean manufacturing.
11. Kansei Engineering — an approach that focuses on capturing customer emotional feedback about products to drive improvement.
12. TQM — total quality management is a management strategy aimed at embedding awareness of quality in all organizational processes. First promoted in Japan with the Deming prize which was adopted and adapted in USA as the Malcolm Baldrige National Quality Award and in Europe as the European Foundation for Quality Management award (each with their own variations).
13. TRIZ — meaning "theory of inventive problem solving"
14. BPR — business process reengineering, a management approach aiming at optimizing the workflows and processes within an organisation.

15. OQRM — Object-oriented Quality and Risk Management, a model for quality and risk management.
16. EcoMobility SHIFT, a tool to assess, audit and label urban transport performance in cities.

Proponents of each approach have sought to improve them as well as apply them for small, medium and large gains. Simple one is Process Approach, which forms the basis of ISO 9001:2008 Quality Management System standard, duly driven from the 'Eight principles of Quality management', process approach being one of them.

Thareja writes about the mechanism and benefits: "The process (proficiency) may be limited in words, but not in its applicability. While it fulfills the criteria of all-round gains: in terms of the competencies augmented by the participants; the organisation seeks newer directions to the business success, the individual brand image of both the people and the organisation, in turn, goes up.

The competencies which were hitherto rated as being smaller, are better recognized and now acclaimed to be more potent and fruitful".[8] The more complex Quality improvement tools are tailored for enterprise types not originally targeted.

For example, Six Sigma was designed for manufacturing but has spread to service enterprises. Each of these approaches and methods has met with success but also with failures.

Some of the common differentiators between success and failure include commitment, knowledge and expertise to guide improvement, scope of change/improvement desired (Big Bang type changes tend to fail more often compared to smaller changes) and adaption to enterprise cultures.

For example, quality circles do not work well in every enterprise (and are even discouraged by some managers), and relatively few TQM-participating enterprises have won the national quality awards.

There have been well publicized failures of BPR, as well as Six Sigma. Enterprises therefore need to consider carefully which quality improvement methods to adopt, and certainly should not adopt all those listed here.

It is important not to underestimate the people factors, such as culture, in selecting a quality improvement approach. Any improvement (change) takes time to implement, gain acceptance and stabilize as accepted practice.

Improvement must allow pauses between implementing new changes so that the change is stabilized and assessed as a real improvement, before the next improvement is made (hence continual improvement, not continuous improvement).

Improvements that change the culture take longer as they have to overcome greater resistance to change. It is easier and often more effective to work within the existing cultural boundaries and make small improvements (that is **Kaizen**) than to make major transformational changes.

Use of Kaizen in Japan was a major reason for the creation of Japanese industrial and economic strength.

On the other hand, transformational change works best when an enterprise faces a crisis and needs to make major changes in order to survive.

In Japan, the land of Kaizen, Carlos Ghosn led a transformational change at Nissan Motor Company which was in a financial and operational crisis.

 Well organized quality improvement programs take all these factors into account when selecting the quality improvement methods.

Quality standards

The International Organization for Standardization (ISO) created the Quality Management System (QMS) standards in 1987. They were the ISO 9000:1987 series of standards comprising ISO 9001:1987, ISO 9002:1987 and ISO 9003:1987; which were applicable in different types of industries, based on the type of activity or process: designing, production or service delivery.

The standards are reviewed every few years by the International Organization for Standardization. The version in 1994 was called the ISO 9000:1994 series; consisting of the ISO 9001:1994, 9002:1994 and 9003:1994 versions.

The last major revision was in the year 2008 and the series was called ISO 9000:2000 series. The ISO 9002 and 9003 standards were integrated into one single certifiable standard: ISO 9001:2000. After December 2003, organizations holding ISO 9002 or 9003 standards had to complete a transition to the new standard.

ISO released a minor revision, ISO 9001:2008 on 14 October 2008. It contains no new requirements. Many of the changes were to improve consistency in grammar, facilitating translation of the standard into other languages for use by over 950,000 certified organization in the 175 countries (as at Dec 2007) that use the standard.

The ISO 9004:2009 document gives guidelines for performance improvement over and above the basic standard (ISO 9001:2000). This standard provides a measurement framework for improved quality management, similar to and based upon the measurement framework for process assessment.

The Quality Management System standards created by ISO are meant to certify the processes and the system of an organization, not the product or service itself. ISO 9000 standards do not certify the quality of the product or service.

In 2005 the International Organization for Standardization released a standard, ISO 22000, meant for the food industry. This standard covers the values and principles of ISO 9000 and the HACCP standards. It gives one single integrated standard for the food industry and is expected to become more popular in the coming years in such industry.

ISO has also released standards for other industries. For example Technical Standard TS 16949 defines requirements in addition to those in ISO 9001:2008 specifically for the automotive industry.

ISO has a number of standards that support quality management. One group describes processes (including ISO/IEC 12207 & ISO/IEC 15288) and another describes process assessment and improvement ISO 15504.

The Software Engineering Institute has its own process assessment and improvement methods, called CMMi (Capability Maturity Model — integrated) and IDEAL respectively

SAFETY MANAGEMENT SYSTEMS

Safety management system (SMS) is a term used to refer to a comprehensive business management system designed to manage safety elements in the workplace.

Description of SMS

A SMS provides a systematic way to identify hazards and control risks while maintaining assurance that these risk controls are effective. SMS can be defined as:

...a businesslike approach to safety. It is a systematic, explicit and comprehensive process for managing safety risks.

As with all management systems, a safety management system provides for goal setting, planning, and measuring performance.

A safety management system is woven into the fabric of an organization. It becomes part of the culture, the way people do their jobs.

For the purposes of defining safety management, safety can be defined as:

... the reduction of risk to a level that is as low as is reasonably practicable.

There are three imperatives for adopting a safety management system for a business – these are ethical, legal and financial.

There is an implied moral obligation placed on an employer to ensure that work activities and the place of work to be safe, there are legislative requirements defined in just about every jurisdiction on how this is to be achieved and there is a substantial body of research which shows that effective safety management (which is the reduction of risk in the workplace) can reduce the financial exposure of an organisation by reducing direct and indirect costs associated with accident and incidents.

To address these three important elements, an effective SMS should:

- Define how the organisation is set up to manage risk.
- Identify workplace risk and implement suitable controls.
- Implement effective communications across all levels of the organisation.
- Implement a process to identify and correct non-conformities.
- Implement a continual improvement process.

A safety management system can be created to fit any business type and/or industry sector.

Basic safety-management components

International Labour Organisation SMS model

Since there are many models to choose from to outline the basic components of a safety management system, the one chosen here is the international standard promoted by the International Labour Organisation (ILO). In the ILO document ILO-OSH 2001 Guidelines on Occupational Safety and Health Management Systems, the safety management basic components are:

- Policy
- Organizing
- Planning and implementation
- Evaluation
- Action for improvement

Although other SMS models use different terminology, the process and workflow for safety management systems is always the same;

1. Policy – Establish within policy statements what the requirements are for the organisation in terms of resources, defining management commitment and defining OSH targets
2. Organizing – How is the organisation structured, where are responsibilities and accountabilities defined, who reports to who and who is responsible for what.
3. Planning and Implementation – What legislation and standards apply to our organisation, what OSH objectives are defined and how are these reviews, hazard prevention and the assessment and management of risk.
4. Evaluation – How is OSH performance measured and assessed, what are the processes for the reporting of accidents and incidents and for the

investigation of accidents and what internal and external audit processes are in place to review the system.

5. Action for Improvement – How are preventative and corrective actions managed and what processes are in place to ensure the continual improvement process. There is a significant amount of detail within each of these sections and these should be examined in detail from the ILO-OSH Guidelines document.

SIX SIGMA

6σ

- **Six Sigma** is a set of techniques and tools for process improvement. It was developed by Motorola in 1986, coinciding with the Japanese asset price bubble which is reflected in its terminology.
- Six Sigma became famous when Jack Welch made it central to his successful business strategy at General Electric in 1995. Today, it is used in many industrial sectors.
- Six Sigma seeks to improve the quality of process outputs by identifying and removing the causes of defects (errors) and minimizing variability in manufacturing and business processes.
- It uses a set of quality management methods, including statistical methods, and creates a special infrastructure of people within the organization ("Champions", "Black Belts", "Green Belts", "Yellow Belts", etc.) who are experts in the methods.
- Each Six Sigma project carried out within an organization follows a defined sequence of steps and has quantified value targets, for example: reduce process cycle time, reduce pollution, reduce costs, increase customer satisfaction, and increase profits.
- The term *Six Sigma* originated from terminology associated with **manufacturing**, specifically terms associated with statistical modeling of manufacturing processes.
- The maturity of a manufacturing process can be described by a *sigma* rating indicating its yield or the percentage of defect-free products it creates.
- A six sigma process is one in which 99.99966% of the products manufactured are statistically expected to be free of defects (3.4 defective parts/million), although, as discussed below, this defect level corresponds to only a 4.5 sigma level.
- Motorola set a goal of "six sigma" for all of its manufacturing operations, and this goal became a by-word for the management and engineering practices used to achieve it.
- **Origin and meaning of the term "six sigma process"**
- The term "six sigma process" comes from the notion that if one has six standard deviations between the process mean and the nearest

specification limit, as shown in the graph, practically no items will fail to meet specifications. This is based on the calculation method employed in process capability studies.

- Capability studies measure the number of standard deviations between the process mean and the nearest specification limit in sigma units, represented by the Greek letter σ (sigma). As process standard deviation goes up, or the mean of the process moves away from the center of the tolerance, fewer standard deviations will fit between the mean and the nearest specification limit, decreasing the sigma number and increasing the likelihood of items outside specification.

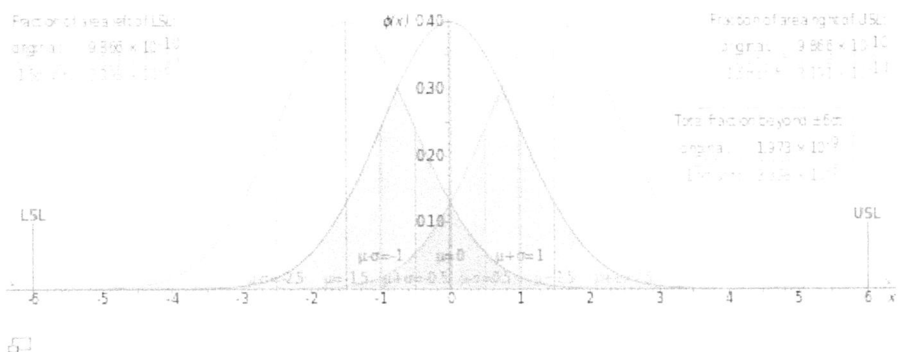

- Graph of the normal distribution, which underlies the statistical assumptions of the Six Sigma model.
- The Greek letter σ (sigma) marks the distance on the horizontal axis between the mean, μ, and the curve's inflection po nt.
- The greater this distance, the greater is the spread of values encountered. For the green curve shown above, μ = 0 and σ = 1. The upper and lower specification limits (USL and LSL, respectively) are at a distance of 6σ from the mean.
- Because of the properties of the normal distribution, values lying that far away from the mean are extremely unlikely. Even if the mean were to move right or left by 1.5σ at some point in the future (1.5 sigma shift, coloured red and blue), there is still a good safety cushion.

- This is why Six Sigma aims to have processes where the mean is at most 6σ away from the nearest specification limit.

<u>STATISTICAL QUALITY CONTROL</u>

Statistical quality control (SQC)

The application of statistical techniques to measure and evaluate the quality of a product, service, or process.

Two basic categories:

I. Statistical process control (SPC):

- the application of statistical techniques to determine whether a process is functioning as desired

II. Acceptance Sampling:

- the application of statistical techniques to determine whether a population of items should be accepted or rejected based on inspection of a sample of those items.

Quality Measurement: Attributes vs Variables

Attributes:

Characteristics that are measured as either "acceptable" or "not acceptable", thus have only discrete, binary, or integer values.

Variables:

Characteristics that are measured on a continuous scale.

Statistical Process Control (SPC) Methods

Statistical process control (SPC) monitors specified quality characteristics of a product or service so as:

To detect whether the process has changed in a way that will affect product quality and

To measure the current quality of products or services.

Control is maintained through the use of control charts. The charts have upper and lower control limits and the process is in

control if sample measurements are between the limits.

Control Charts for Attributes

P Charts - measures proportion defective.

C Charts - measures the number of defects/unit.

Control Charts for Variables

X bar and R charts are used together - control a process by ensuring that the sample average and range remain within

limits for both.

Basic Procedure

1. An upper control limit (UCL) and a lower control limit (LCL) are set for the process.

2. A random sample of the product or service is taken, and the specified quality characteristic is measured.

3. If the average of the sample of the quality characteristic is higher than the upper control limit or lower than the lower control limit, the process is considered to be "out of control".

CONTROL CHARTS FOR ATTRIBUTES

p-Charts for Proportion Defective

p-chart: a statistical control chart that plots movement in the sample proportion defective (p) over time

Procedure:

1. take a random sample and inspect each item

2. determine the sample proportion defective by dividing the number of defective items by the sample size

3. plot the sample proportion defective on the control chart and compare with UCL and LCL to determine if process is out of control

The underlying statistical sampling distribution is the binomial distribution, but can be approximated by the normal distribution with:

mean = u = np **(Note - add the bars above the means used in all the equations in this section)**

standard deviation of p: **sigma$_p$** = square root of (p(1 -p) / n)

where p = historical population **proportion defective** and n = sample size

Control Limits:

UCL = u + z sigma$_p$

LCL = u - z sigma $_p$

z is the number of standard deviations from the mean. It is set based how certain you wish to be that when a limit is exceeded it is due to a change in the process proportion defective rather than due to sample variability. For example:

If z = 1 if p has not changed you will still exceed the limits in 32% of the samples (68% confident that mean has changed if the limits are exceeded.

z = 2 - limits will be exceeded in 4.5 (95.5 % confidence that mean has changed)

z = 3 - limits will be exceeded in .03 (99.7% confidence)

c-Charts for Number of Defects Per Unit

c-chart: a statistical control chart that plots movement in the number of defects per unit.

Procedure:

1. randomly select one item and count the number of defects in that item

2. plot the number of defects on a control chart

3. compare with UCL and LCL to determine if process is out of control

The underlying sampling distribution is the Poisson distribution, but can be approximated by the normal distribution with: **mean = c**

standard deviation = square root of c

where c is the historical average number of **defects/unit**

Control Limits:

UCL = c + z c

LCL = c - z c

CONTROL CHARTS FOR VARIABLES

Two charts are used together: **R-chart ("range chart") and X barchart ("average chart")**

Both the process variability (measured by the R-chart) and the process average (measured by the X bar chart) must be in control before the process can be said to be in control.

Process variability must be in control before the X bar chart can be developed because a measure of process variability is required to determine the -chart control limits.

R-Chart for Process Variability:

$UCL_R = D_4(R)$

$LCL_R = D_3(R)$

where is the average of past R values, and D_3 and D_4 are constants based on the sample size

-Chart for Process Average:

$UCLR = X\ bar + A_2(R)$

$LCL = X\ bar - A_2(R)$

where X bar is the average of several past values, and A_2 is a constant based on the sample size

OTHER TYPES OF ATTRIBUTE-SAMPLING PLANS

Double-Sampling Plan:

Specifies two sample sizes (n_1 and n_2) and two acceptance levels (c_1 and c_2)

1. if the first sample passes (actual defects c_1), the lot is accepted

2. if the first sample fails and actual defects $> c_2$, the lot is rejected

3. if first sample fails but $c_1 <$ actual defects c_2, the second sample is taken and judged on the combined number of defectives found.

Sequential-Sampling Plan:

Each time an item is inspected, a decision is made whether to accept the lot, reject it, or continue sampling.

<u>TOTAL QUALITY MANAGEMENT (TQM)</u>

A core definition of total quality management (TQM) describes a management approach to long–term success through customer satisfaction.

In a TQM effort, all members of an organization participate in improving processes, products, services, and the culture in which they work.

The methods for implementing this approach come from the teachings of such quality leaders as **Philip B. Crosby**, **W. Edwards Deming**, **Armand V. Feigenbaum**, **Kaoru Ishikawa**, and **Joseph M. Juran**.

The Primary Elements of TQM

Total quality management can be summarized as a management system for a customer-focused organization that involves all employees in continual improvement. It uses strategy, data, and effective communications to integrate the quality discipline into the culture and activities of the organization.

- **Customer-focused**. The customer ultimately determines the level of quality. No matter what an organization does to foster quality improvement—training employees, integrating quality into the design process, upgrading computers or software, or buying new measuring tools—the customer determines whether the efforts were worthwhile.

- **Total employee involvement**. All employees participate in working toward common goals. Total employee commitment can only be obtained after fear has been driven from the workplace, when empowerment has occurred, and management has provided the proper environment. High-performance work systems integrate continuous improvement efforts with normal business operations. Self-managed work teams are one form of empowerment.

- **Process-centered**. A fundamental part of TQM is a focus on process thinking. A process is a series of steps that take inputs from suppliers (internal or external) and transforms them into outputs that are delivered to customers (again, either internal or external). The steps required to carry out the process are defined, and performance measures are continuously monitored in order to detect unexpected variation.

- **Integrated system**. Although an organization may consist of many different functional specialties often organized into vertically structured departments, it is the horizontal processes interconnecting these functions that are the focus of TQM.
    - Micro-processes add up to larger processes, and all processes aggregate into the business processes required for defining and implementing strategy. Everyone must understand the vision, mission, and guiding principles as well as the quality policies, objectives, and critical processes of the organization. Business performance must be monitored and communicated continuously.
    - An integrated business system may be modeled after the Baldrige National Quality Program criteria and/or incorporate the ISO 9000 standards. Every organization has a unique work culture, and it is virtually impossible to achieve excellence in its products and services unless a good quality culture has been fostered. Thus, an integrated system connects business improvement elements in an attempt to continually improve and exceed the expectations of customers, employees, and other stakeholders.

- **Strategic and systematic approach**. A critical part of the management of quality is the strategic and systematic approach to achieving an organization's vision, mission, and goals. This process, called strategic planning or strategic management, includes the formulation of a strategic plan that integrates quality as a core component.

- **Continual improvement**. A major thrust of TQM is continual process improvement. Continual improvement drives an organization to be both analytical and creative in finding ways to become more competitive and more effective at meeting stakeholder expectations.

- **Fact-based decision making**. In order to know how well an organization is performing, data on performance measures are necessary. TQM requires that an organization continually collect and analyze data in order to improve decision making accuracy, achieve consensus, and allow prediction based on past history.

- **Communications**. During times of organizational change, as well as part of day-to-day operation, effective communications plays a large part in maintaining morale and in motivating employees at all levels. Communications involve strategies, method, and timeliness.